CW01510964

Zambia:
The Land and Its People

Godfrey Mwakikagile

Copyright (c) 2010 Zambia: The Land and Its People
All rights reserved.

Zambia: The Land and Its People
Godfrey Mwakikagile

First Edition

ISBN 978-9987-9322-5-2

Continental Press
Dar es Salaam, Tanzania

traditions
& example
p. 86
"rain ritual"

unifying factor
in Zambia; but
also opportunity
to express needs
towards
government

local vs.
central
decision
making
p. 91!

chieftan
p. 94/134
100/134

peaceful
[?] problems
with
Congo
p. 98
many refugees/
militaria invading
etc.

- conflict btw.
district + central
government
p. 73 - modernisation
of Chienge district

- urbanised areas - but also
very rural districts without proper
infrastructure/electricity or telephone

(Luapula
Province/
or even
in the
opposite-
the most
urbanised
province
in Zambia
(Lufunyama
district)

DEMOCRATIC REPUBLIC OF THE CONGO
TANZANIA
Lake Tanganyika
Lake Mweru
Mpulungu
Kasama
Mafinga Hills
Lake Bangweulu
Luapula
ANGOLA
Solwezi
Mufulira
Kitwe
Ndola
Kapiri Mposhi
Chipata
MAL.
Kabwe
Mongu
LUSAKA
Zambezi
Lake Kariba
MOZ.
NAMIBIA
Livingstone
ZIMBABWE
BOTSWANA
0   100   200 km
0   100   200 mi

Scott Taylor: Culture &
Customs of Zambia

- highly reliable on
agriculture

3

▷ main appeals towards government
regard Infrastructure (construction or
improvement of roads); agricultural support
electricity
(fertiliser / training) or security (especially in
interior); always direct your appeal towards (also)
government

   ⤷ government strongly perceived as kind
    of "service provider"

p.101; 73; 86; 102 ⤷ mainly the role of
  154 _____ the chief

⌈ high diversity of interests / chiefs mainly
seek support for their area in terms of
infrastructure, agriculture & economic
support ⌉⌉

⌈ Interesting note – it's always "the government"
not the department or Minister" that is held
responsible or is addressed ⌉⌉

_____

local district offices are often short on funds
and partly poor
   ⤷ e.g. Mr ⌈Ohana Council (→ funds are
gone by mid year ⌉⌉
_____

p.120 – Empowering clause ?

4

Health - 114 e.g.
└ poor health services; many towns without hospital; prevalence of traditional healers esp. in rural areas

Interesting: Dio are as political active group - ph Siluezi

└ Western Province Secerianist tendencies p. 149 ff

Contents

Introduction

Part One:
Zambia:
General Background

Part Two:
The Land

Part Three:
Provinces

Part Four:
Major Towns and Cities

How many chiefs? local participation? vs logistics?

Introduction

THIS work is a general introduction to Zambia. It does not pretend to be a scholarly work or an in-depth study of this African country. It's a simple presentation of some basic facts, and some analysis here and there, about one of the most stable and peaceful countries on the continent.

Many people outside Africa don't know about Zambia. You find more people who know about Nigeria, Kenya, Ethiopia, South Africa and a few other African countries than they do about Zambia.

One of the main reasons many people don't know about this African country is its history of relative peace and stability since independence almost 50 years ago.

Many African countries have been wracked by violence in varying degrees through the decades. Only a few have been spared this agony on a continent where civil strife is the norm rather than the exception. One of those few exceptions is Zambia.

In fact, it's now part of conventional wisdom to view Africa as a turbulent continent where peace is rare or nonexistent. In many cases, this is a stereotype. As Julius Nyerere, president of Tanzania, once said: "The only time you hear about peace in Africa is when it is broken."

But it is equally true that this stereotypical image of Africa is a reflection of reality in many cases, especially when you look at the number of countries which have been torn by violence through the decades since independence in the sixties. Even as recently as the 1990s, more than 30 African countries – out of 53 – were affected by civil strife, including civil wars, which even destroyed some of them.

Therefore, it is quite an achievement for a few countries such as Zambia to have been able to maintain peace and stability in the midst of chaos for decades since independence.

A number of people, including Africans themselves, have written books about this horrendous tragedy. They include well-known writers such as Wole Soyinka whose blistering attack on the leadership in his home country was given forceful expression in one of his books, *The Open Sore of a Continent: A Personal Narrative of the Nigerian Crisis*; Chinua Achebe, another luminary and literary giant, in his book, *The Trouble with Nigeria*; and less well-known ones such as George Ayittey, *Africa in Chaos*; and Godfrey Mwakikagile, *Africa is in A Mess: What Went Wrong and What Should be Done*.

The first three writers are West Africans. And the last one is an East African, from Tanzania, a country that borders Zambia. Coincidentally, he also comes from a region – Mbeya Region – in southwestern Tanzania which borders Zambia and some of whose people straddle the Tanzanian-Zambian border.

While all these writers have written about the chaos, trials and tribulations which are virtually synonymous with the name of "Africa," not as many have written about the peace and stability which prevails in a number of countries such as Zambia. Many people have never even heard of

Zambia.

I am not an expert on the political dynamics which have shaped Zambia since independence. But I have some knowledge of the country to help members of the general public – who don't know anything or who know very little about Zambia – learn quite a few things about this young and dynamic African nation in the heart of southern Africa.

Therefore members of the general public, including tourists, may find this work to be useful. It may even help some students learn some of the things they don't know about Zambia, but bearing in mind that this work is not an in-depth study of this African country. If it's going to help some people, and if it's going to encourage others to learn more about Zambia, it will have achieved its purpose.

It has its faults, like all works by mere mortals, but at least it does not pretend to be a definitive or a comprehensive – let alone a scholarly – work on Zambia. But I believe it's comprehensive enough as an introductory work on this magnificent land and its people.

Welcome to Zambia.

Part One:

Zambia: General Background

ZAMBIA is located in southern Africa, although it's sometimes considered to be a part of East Africa. The name "Zambia" is derived from the Zambezi River.

Almost an entire half of the country is geographically a part of what is considered to be the eastern region of Africa.

But most of the time, Zambia is considered to be a part of southern Africa. And historically, it has always been considered to be a part of southern Africa because of its colonial heritage which links it to what is now Zimbabwe. During British colonial rule, Zambia was known as Northern Rhodesia. And what is Zimbabwe today was called Southern Rhodesia.

The area that is now known as Zambia was once

inhabited by the members of the Khoisan groups. They moved from place to place, hunting and gathering fruits, roots and other edible items for their survival. And they lived in this area for centuries.

Then during the first centuries A.D., members of other tribes moved into the region. They came from what is now Congo and from some parts of the Great Lakes region of East Africa. But they came mostly from the Congo region.

They were of Bantu stock and had, centuries earlier, migrated from West Africa, especially in the region which is now eastern Nigeria and Cameroon.

The members of Bantu tribes were mostly farmers. When they entered the area that is now Zambia, they encountered the Khoisan whom they overpowered. The Khoisan gradually left and sought new homelands in the southern part of Africa.

But some members of the Khoisan groups stayed and gradually became a part of the Bantu communities. They intermarried with them and lost their identity because they were overwhelmed by sheer numbers and by the dominant Bantu cultures.

The migration of Bantus into the region continued through the centuries and reached its peak in the 1300s A.D.

Members of the Tonga tribe are believed to be the first Bantu group to settle in what is now Zambia. They migrated into the region from the east and are believed to have left their home in the Great Lakes region.

The Great Lakes region is known as the continent's main lake region. The three largest lakes in Africa are in this region. They are Lake Victoria, the largest on the continent and the second-largest freshwater lake in the world after Lake Superior in North America; Lake Nyasa; and Lake Tanganyika which is the second-deepest lake in the world after Lake Baikal in Russia.

Other groups which migrated into what is now Zambia came from the Luba and Lunda tribes. The Luba and the

Lunda are the largest ethnic groups in the southern part of the Democratic Republic of Congo (DRC). Some of them also live in northern Angola.

There was another wave of immigrants which entered the area. These were the Ngoni and the Sotho who migrated from South Africa in the 1800s, contributing to the ethnic and cultural diversity of what is now Zambia.

As the 1800s came to an end, the demographic landscape of the area had already been shaped, with each of the ethnic groups having established a homeland. The areas are still the homelands of the tribes in Zambia today, each having a clear ethnic and cultural identity.

But they were soon to lose their freedom and independence to imperial rulers. The pioneer of this imperial conquest was Cecil Rhodes. He was the leader of the British South Africa Company (BSAC) and entered the region in search of minerals but also with territorial ambitions to establish a British colony.

The first success he had was when he convinced King Lewanika of the Lozi – also known as Baratose – to sign a treaty in 1890 giving him mineral rights in the land of these indigenous people in the western part of the country. This eventually led to the establishment of a colonial territory that later came to be known as North-Western Rhodesia. The colonial entity was established in 1891 under the charter of the British South Africa Company.

The British South Africa Company also established control in the eastern part of the country. The eastern part was inhabited by the members of the Ngoni tribe who had migrated to region from Natal in South Africa.

The Ngoni tried to resist this imperial incursion and put up a stiff defence under their leader, Mpezeni, but they lost. The British South Africa Company went on to seize this territory and named it North-Eastern Rhodesia.

For a period, the two colonial territories were administer as separate entities. But they were both British imperial possessions under the same leadership.

The two territories were merged in 1911 to form one colony. The merger was facilitated by the British South Africa Company and the new colony was named Northern Rhodesia.

Kalomo, a town in the southern part of the country, became the first administrative centre – or capital – of the colony of Northern Rhodesia.

The capital was moved to Livingstone between 1907 and 1911. Livingstone is also in the southern part of the country and was named in honour of the missionary-doctor-explorer David Livingstone.

In 1923, the British South Africa Company lost control of Northern Rhodesia when the British Government refused to extend the company's mandate. It revoked the company's charter.

It was also in the same year, 1923, that Southern Rhodesia – now Zimbabwe – which was also administered by the British South Africa Company, became a self-governing territory, giving substantial powers to the white minority settlers over the black majority in that country.

In August 1953, the British colonial settlers established the Federation of Rhodesia and Nyasaland. It comprised Northern Rhodesia, Southern Rhodesia, and Nyasaland which was renamed Malawi after independence. The union was also known as the Central African Federation.

Many Africans, especially the nationalists, in all the three countries – of Northern Rhodesia, Southern Rhodesia and Nyasaland – were opposed to the establishment of the federation. Like their counterparts in East Africa – Kenya, Uganda and Tanganyika – who were also strongly opposed to the establishment of an East African federation by the British rulers, they felt that the Federation of Rhodesia and Nyasaland would consolidate white domination.

But the white settlers ignored them. They intended to declare independence one day, excluding the black majority.

The federation of Rhodesia and Nyasaland was dissolved in December 1963 under sustained opposition by black African nationalists. It was the dawn of a new era which finally led to independence in the territories involved.

Formation of another federation, on terms stipulated by Africans, was proposed years later by Zambian President Kenneth Kaunda when he said Zambia and the newly independent Zimbabwe should unite under one federal government. According to a report, "Zambia, Zimbabwe Federation Can Defeat Western Influence," in *The Herald*, Harare, Zimbabwe:

"In April 1980, Zambia's founding president Dr Kenneth Kaunda made a stunning proposal on strengthening the economic power of Zambia and Zimbabwe following the latter's attainment of political independence on April 18 of that year.

Dr Kaunda proposed a federation of Zambia and Zimbabwe. This was stunning because Dr Kaunda had, as a matter of fact, proposed to be the federal foreign minister with President Mugabe as president.

This was unprecedented in Africa and would by today have countered the west's attempted siege on Zimbabwe.

Zambia, Zimbabwe and Malawi were from 1953 to 1963 a federation with the capital at Salisbury, now Harare with Great Britain pulling the strings from Lancaster House.

The Federation's resources were channelled to Salisbury and London to be enjoyed by the white minority.

When Independent Zambia and Malawi broke the back of the federation, Ian Douglas Smith then Rhodesian prime minister made his Unilateral Declaration of Independence on November 11 1965, isolating his minority regime from Britain and to an extent the rest of the world, save for apartheid South Africa.

In revisiting Dr Kaunda's proposal during an interview

with a foreign correspondent in Lusaka, one must look at the history and the current situation existing in the sub-region vis-à-vis western powers, particularly the USA and Britain.

The cause of the current problems in Zimbabwe is that the Government of Zimbabwe under Zanu-PF and President Mugabe reclaimed, without compensation, land from the descendants of Rhodesian settlers who had, in the 18th century kicked out indigenous Zimbabweans from prime land and kept it for themselves and their descendants

On the eve of Zimbabwe's independence, the stakeholders in the then Zimbabwe-Rhodesia including the liberation movements, Zanla and Zipra, held discussions mediated by Britain at Lancaster House agreeing, among other things, that Britain would compensate white commercial farmers once time came to empower indigenous Zimbabweans.

In November 1997, November 5 to be specific, Britain abrogated its promises and President Mugabe had to act to fulfil his pledge to give people the land so many had died for, and as soon as that happened the British government of Tony Blair joined by their American cousins ran amok accusing President Mugabe of human rights abuses and initiated sanctions that have been choking Zimbabwe.

Suffice to say the Zimbabwean opposition backed by some western governments and economic refugees in the Diaspora have created an untenable international situation for the survival of Zimbabwe.

There is need to revisit Dr Kaunda's foresight into today's political and economic situation.

When it comes to wisdom, even though I have an advanced western education, I am a Kaundaist at heart and will never apologise to anyone.

Dr Kaunda, at the inception of Zimbabwe's independence foresaw the loss of many qualified exiles that had become Zambian residents from journalists, nurses, security personnel to doctors and civil servants who left a big vacuum in Zambia as they trekked back to rebuild Zimbabwe. Had anyone then decided to take that challenging proposal, I doubt if at all the prevailing economic situation would have been as it is today. I might add too that a federated Zambia and Zimbabwe would have been a power block to reckon with because:

There would have been a continuity of a well-groomed civil service in both countries.

There would have been enough land to go between the native peoples and the descendants of white settlers. A lot of whites who lost their land in Zimbabwe have settled in the Zambian Mkushi farming block.

There would have been a very healthy and competitive political spirit in the federation, judging by the good parliamentary democracy existing in both countries today.

The points above would have negated the hostility exhibited by big brother Britain and United States.

In numbers we have strength and that is what the federation would have brought and can still bring. Vast natural resources exist in Zambia and Zimbabwe that would satisfy all the citizens without recourse to big brothers.

The spirit of unity in Sadc and to a greater extent the African Union that has been shown by men like Presidents Levy Mwanawasa, and Thabo Mbeki to stand by Zimbabwe internationally should any international power try to divide us by refusing to invite President Mugabe to the forthcoming EU-Africa summit, goes a long way in showing how as one common people, Zambians and Zimbabweans can form a perfect union that takes them out of the prevailing economic malaise.

President Mugabe and Zanu-PF, now remain the more serious and mature party politically in an envisaged federal government and thus, the onus remains on them to spearhead the formation of the federation as proposed by Dr Kaunda years ago.

The benefits would be immense and would render big brother's tactics against Zimbabwe impotent. A new regional power in the mould of South Africa would emerge and there is no telling the growth of opportunity in all areas that would benefit the people and Africa in particular.

Let us take up the challenge and form the Federation of Zambia and Zimbabwe now, posterity will hold us in high esteem!" – (Allan S. Mulenga, "Zambia, Zimbabwe Federation Can Defeat Western Influence," in *The Herald*, Harare, Zimbabwe, 16 October 2007).

The dissolution of the white-dominated Central African Federation helped pave the way for the independence of its constituent territories, Nyasaland and Northern Rhodesia, with the exception of Southern Rhodesia whose liberation came years later in April 1980 after a bloody guerrilla warfare against white minority rule.

In the case of Northern Rhodesia, the country became independent on 24 October 1964 and changed its name to Zambia.

Zambia is a landlocked country. It's bordered by the Democratic Republic of Congo (DRC) on the north; by Tanzania on the northeast, Malawi on the east, Mozambique on the southeast; by Zimbabwe on the south and southeast; by Botswana on the south, Namibia on the southwest, and by Angola on the west.

The capital of Zambia is Lusaka. It's located in the southeastern part of the country. During the liberation struggle against white minority governments in the countries of southern Africa, Lusaka served as an operational base for the liberation movements, together with Dar es Salaam, the capital of neighbouring Tanzania which was the headquarters of all the liberation movements in Africa during that period.

Zambia had a population of about 13 million in 2009 in an area of 290,587 square miles.

The majority of the people live around Lusaka and in a region known as the Copperbelt which is located in the northwestern part of the country.

The official language of Zambia is English. Other major languages are Nyanja, Bemba, Lunda, Tonga, Lozi, Kaonde and Luvale. They are mostly regional languages, although many people who speak these languages also live in different parts of the country, especially in the towns and cities.

Urbanisation, especially since the 1950s, the decade before independence, has played a big role in this demographic change and reconfiguration.

The transformation has had a profound impact on Zambian national life and culture, compounded by foreign influences which have introduced new values and ideas, as well as life styles unheard of before.

Old tribal ways remain strong even in towns and cities. But they have come increasing pressure from foreign influence.

Even influences from other African countries have had a negative impact on Zambia's cultural life. For example, interest in Congolese music is so widespread that indigenous music now plays a subordinate role among many Zambians especially those who live in towns and cities cross the country.

Interest in foreign culture and material things, especially from the industrialised and "civilised" West, also has had negative consequences. For example, growth in the second-hand clothing industry, known as *salaula* in Zambia, has had a profound effect on the domestic clothing industry. It has almost destroyed it. The term *salaula* means "to rummage through a pile."

The term refers to the bundled used clothing obtained from developed countries, especially those in the West mainly the United States, Britain, Canada and others such as Germany, Sweden, Denmark, Belgium and France.

There is genuine demand for clothes. But, also, there is

no question that many people prefer to wear, and they want to be seen wearing, Western clothes, because it makes them look more "civilised" than their brethren who don't have or can't afford those kinds of clothes.

It's mental slavery.

Even in matters of language, many educated Zambians prefer English, ignoring their tribal languages which they consider to be beneath them and good only for "illiterates" especially those in the rural areas.

Aware of this threat to their cultural integrity, many Zambians, including government officials encourage their fellow countrymen to be proud of their cultures – tribal customs and traditions – and their African way of life.

The government has even launched initiatives to preserve, protect and promote tribal cultures which collectively constitute the nation's cultural diversity. For example, the *kuomboka* traditional ceremony of the Lozi people of western Zambia is one of the practices which has been accorded attention by the government as a cultural institution worth of preservation.

The word *kuomboka*, in the Lozi language, literally means "to get out of water." In my Nyakyusa language spoken mostly in southwestern Tanzania and by many Nyakyusas in the Cooperbelt Province and elsewhere in Zambia, the term for that is *kuloboka* which literally means "to cross." This striking similarity is typical of Bantu languages because of their common origin.

The term *kuomboka* among the Lozi is used to describe a cultural event which takes place at the end of the rain season when the waters of the upper Zambezi River cover the plains of the Western Province of Zambia in a big flood, making it very difficult and sometimes almost impossible for people to move freely.

The event is a traditional ceremony which involves royal movement. The king of the Lozi, who is known as the *Litunga*, literally moves from his royal compound at Lealui in the Barotse Floodplain of the Zambezi River to

Limulunga, his second royal residence which is on higher and safer ground away from the flood.

This cultural event involves a lot of drumming which takes place before the king relocates. The drumming takes place around the royal residence the day before the ceremony and is intended to announce the coming of *kuomboka* the next day.

The *litunga* is carried on a barge called Nalikwanda. The barge bears the official seal of Zambia: coat of arms with black and white colours.

The barge also carries a large figure of a black elephant whose ears can be manipulated by the people on the barge. The barge also has a fire which is highly symbolic in the culture of the Lozi. Its significance is also directly related to the institution of the monarchy.

The smoke from the fire is intended to signify something very important to the Lozi as a cultural and ethnic entity. It also tells the people that their king, the *litunga*, is still in full control and in good health.

The king's barge is accompanied by another one for his his wife. The wife's barge carries a very large cattle egret called Nalwange. The egret also elephant features. Its wings can be easily manipulated to move up and down like the ears of an elephant.

These are some of the most prominent symbols of the *kuomboka* ceremony.

Kuomboka is one of the most important traditional ceremonies in Zambia intended to preserve customs and traditions, and the traditional way of life, among the people across the country.

The promotion and preservation of tribal languages is another area of concern.

Zambia has a number of major tribal languages. But they are not necessarily representative of the country's ethnic composition.

There are at least 75 different ethnic groups in Zambia but only seven major tribal languages. These languages are

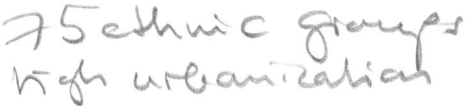
75 ethnic groups
high urbanization

also identified with particular ethnic groups which are regionally entrenched.

The large number of ethnic groups in Zambia is one of the most remarkable features of this country.

It's a land of remarkable contrasts in terms of geography, culture, life, social and political institutions, social and economic conditions as well as history and demographic composition. As Scott D. Taylor states in his book, *Culture and Customs of Zambia*:

"The country is also one of the most urbanized in sub-Saharan Africa, a phenomenon that began with the colonial era gravitation toward the central mining regions of Zambia's Copperbelt.

As a result of this urban influx, Zambia's diverse ethnolinguistic groups interact regularly. Moreover, many contemporary Zambian households, especially those in cities, are also exposed to the media, technology, and influences of Western urbanized cultures....

In other words, notions of tradition and modernity conflict and combine in interesting ways in contemporary Zambia.

Not surprisingly, for all these reasons, scholars from a variety of disciplines have been fascinated by Zambia's political, economic, and social-development experiences, and the challenges thereto, because the country offers unique insights as well as important lessons for the rest of Africa." - Scott D. Taylor, *Culture and Customs of Zambia*, Santa Barbara, California, USA: Greenwood Press, 2006, p. ix).

While Zambia's unique characteristics provide insights into the country's unique experiences, they equally serve to illuminate themes in other Africa contexts whose relevance is continental in scope because of the striking similarities which are shared by most countries across the continent.

Yet there is a limit to which such similarities can be used as analytical tools in different national contexts because of the differences which exist among these countries.

In the case of Zambia, there is no question that history and geography have interacted in a unique way to produce a nation that exists today but which is also seen as a model for other countries in many areas of national life.

One of those areas is culture where cultural fusion has taken place, cutting across ethno-linguistic boundaries. But there are also situations in which tribal customs are maintained by different groups.

There are also customs which are shared by people of different ethnic groups.

However, in many cases, ethno-linguistic and cultural boundaries are blurred in urban areas which are cosmopolitan in outlook and where loyalty to one's tribe is not as strong as it is in the more conservative rural areas:

"The urban environment has produced an amalgam of traditional and modern where different groups mix socially, linguistically, and in any variety of professional and personal contexts. Thus, the customs in Zambia's urban zones have become increasingly homogenized....

A variety of geographical, historical, and political influences impact culture and customs in Zambia. Interestingly, culture and customs both are undergoing profound changes and revealing important continuities at the same time.

The continued flight to cities, typically in search of employment, for example, has increased citizens' exposure to more Western ideas and influences.

Zambia's recent transition to a more democratic form of government has increased opportunities for social interaction and public expression.

Zambia remains essentially 'Zambian,' however, in the sense that the character of its citizens is unique within the region and within Africa as a whole.

In Zambia today, as in much of Africa, tradition and modernity not only exist side by side, but also what is modern becomes throughly endogenized (sic), and the traditional is altered and adapted as well....

What one sees, then, is a uniquely Zambian combination of elements – in politics, religion, social relations, and so forth.

Culture is inherently fluid, and so it is in Zambia; people adopt new customs and characteristics as a result of exposure to different groups and different customs. Western and other non-Zambian norms are introduced by travel, music, television, and the arts.

Cultural ceremonies die or fade from memory, whereas long-dormant ones are revived and help rekindle a sense of identity, such as the Umutomboko ceremony of the Lunda people.

By the same token, intra-Zambian norms are shared as a result of the inculcation of a thoroughly national identity.

Although this identity was initially imposed artificially through colonialism, a collective sense of so-called Zambianness was later forged out of necessity by President Kaunda and the post-colonial government. Indeed, consider that in precolonial times, the Lozi people had scant knowledge of their Bemba counterparts; today they interact regularly in social, economic and political forums." (Ibid., pp. ix – x).

The creation of this new identity was very much a product of colonialism, not only in Zambia – what was then Northern Rhodesia – but in other parts of Africa as well.

Before the advent of colonial rule, there was no Uganda, Nigeria, Ghana (formerly the Gold Coast), Kenya, Nyasaland (now Malawi), Tanganyika (which became Tanzania after uniting with Zanzibar), Cameroon, Ivory Coast, Southern Rhodesia now Zimbabwe, Gambia, or any of the countries on the continent with the exception of Ethiopia and a few others. It was the imperial powers who created those countries.

But although they divided Africans, they also united them. As Julius Nyerere, the first president of Tanganyika, later Tanzania, stated in 1960 not long before he led Tanganyika to independence from Britain the following year:

"Africans all over the continent, without a word being spoken either from one individual to another or from one African country to another, looked at the European, looked at one another, and knew that in relation to the European they were one." - Julius Nyerere, quoted by Godfrey Mwakikagile, *Africa and The West*, Nova Science Publishers, Inc., Huntington, New York, 2000, p. 70. See also Arthur Hazlewood, editor, *African Integration and Disintegration*, London: Oxford University Press, 1967).

Northern Rhodesia (now Zambia) was no exception. It was an imperial creation.

And this collective sentiment – of the oneness of Africa and Africans – helped to fuel African nationalism in Northern Rhodesia as much as it did in other parts of Africa. As Kenneth Kaunda, the leader of the independence movement in Northern Rhodesia, stated: "Zambia Shall be Free." That was also the title of his book, first published in 1963, just before he led his country to independence in 1964.

And when the country emerged from colonial rule, the task of nation building and consolidation began.

One of the main tasks was to unite the people of different ethnic groups into a cohesive bloc. It is a task that continues today.

And the country has had an impressive record through the decades trying to achieve this goal. There has also been significant cultural interaction, and fusion, as a result

24

merging of cultures → within Zambia
- with external
values

of external influences, producing a unique Zambian identity. As Scott Taylor states:

"Examples abound of the merging of cultures and customs, both intra-Zambian and between Zambian and Western traditions and practices.

Christianity is pervasive, though it incorporates indigenous traditions in some locales; English is the first language of many middle class urban children; traditional, historically secretive wedding rites are now commonly captured on that most essential of modern devices, video; urban dialects of Nyanja and Bemba language are increasingly sprinkled with English words so as to form altogether new speech patterns; the cultural ceremonies of one ethnic group are adopted, modified, and incorporated into those of another – e.g., such that the marriage ritual *amatebeto* becomes a Zambian cultural tradition as much as a Bemba one.

In short, these new customs, habits – indeed, traditions – thus become thoroughly embedded, and the culture adapts to accommodate them.

These are the issues that make the study of the culture and customs of Zambia so compelling and dynamic." - (S. D. Taylor, *Culture and Customs of Zambia*, op.cit., p. xi).

Equally compelling and inspiring are Zambia's other characteristics including physical and geographical features as well as climate. The country is known for its geographic diversity.

It also has abundant fertile land, unlike many other countries on the continent.

Availability of plenty of arable land is one of the main reasons Zambia has been able to maintain peace and stability through the decades since independence, making it possible almost for every Zambian to get some land without fighting for it.

peace → plenty of arable land

Part Two:

The Land

LAND is inextricably linked with life in all societies round the globe but even more so countries such as Zambia and others in the Third World which are heavily dependent on agriculture, unlike industrialised nations.

And a lot has to do with geography, including climate, as well as availability of arable land and other resources such as rivers.

Zambia has all that: plenty of arable land, a good climate conducive to agriculture, and enough water from some of the largest rivers on the African continent. In fact, one of the most important assets Zambia has is its rivers. Millions of people live along the banks of the major rivers such as the Zambezi. And millions more live in the valleys which are sustained by these rivers.

Geography itself has been a blessing to Zambia in terms of life sustenance. The country does not have a harsh climate. It has no desert. It has little barren land.

Zambia is located only a few hundred miles from the equator. It has a tropical climate and consists mostly of high plateau with some hills and mountains, dissected by river valleys.

Therefore, although the climate is tropical, it's not harsh because of the high altitude in much of the country, providing a moderating influence.

In some cases, the geographical contrasts within the country make Zambia unique in the region of southern Africa and on the continent as a whole.

It has the majestic Victoria Falls shared with Zimbabwe. It also has the Zambezi River which starts in the northern part of the country and across the border in the Democratic Republic of Congo (DRC).

The Zambezi is the largest and longest river in southern Africa. It's also one of the largest and longest on the entire continent. It's 2,200 miles long and empties into the Indian Ocean..

Zambia also is home to Kariba Dam, one of the largest dams in the world built in the 1950s. The lake formed by the dam is the largest man-made lake in Africa and in the entire world.

The dam was completed in 1958, forming Lake Kariba. The lake is 1,900 square miles. It's one of the largest artificial lakes in the world.

Zambia has two major river basins. There is the Zambezi basin in the southern part of the country. It covers about 75 per cent of the country's total area. And there is the Congo basin in the north which covers about 25 per cent of Zambia's territory.

In other words, two among the largest rivers on the continent, the Congo and the Zambezi, have a direct impact on life in Zambia.

The Zambezi basin also has some of the largest rivers in Zambia and in Africa. One of these rivers in the Kafue. And it plays a very important role in Zambia's national life including the environment. It not only provides sustenance to millions of people; it also sustains ssome of the world's most important wild life areas.

The Kafue River bisects Zambia and is the most centrally located river in the country. It's also the only river in Zambia with the largest number of urban areas. Many urban centres in Zambia claim the river as an integral part of those areas. It's the longest river in Zambia. And its entire length is also within the country's territorial borders.

The river is an integral part of a number of towns in the Copperbelt Province. It flows within the geographical limits of some of the towns. And in some cases, it's very close to a number of urban areas.

The Kafue River flows through the outer limits Kitwe and Nchanga. It also flows to close to Chingola, Chililabombwe, and Mufulira. All these are major mining centres in the Copperbelt Province which use the Kafue River in a number of areas including provision of water, drainage, fishing, and recreation.

It's a very important means of livelihood in the Copperbelt Province which is also simply known as the Copperbelt. Water from the river is used to irrigate small farms and market gardens which produce vegetables, fruits and other commodities. It's also used for cooking, washing, cleaning, and building. To many people in the Copperbelt Province, the Kafue River is what the Nile is to many Egyptians.

The kafue River also plays a very important role in sustaining the Kafue National Park. It flows through the park. The park is named after the river. It's the largest park in Zambia and is an integral part of three provinces: North Western, Central, and Southern provinces. But it's mainly in the Central Province.

Establishment of the park by th British government in 1924 disrupted the social and economic life of the indigenous people, members of the Nkoya tribe, forcing them to move to other parts. The area where the park was established was the traditional hunting territory for Nkoya tribesmen Expropriation of the land by the colonial rulers was one of the worst injustices perpetrated against the indigenous people and it their disrupted traditional way of life and even institutions.

Even after Northern Rhodesia won independence in 1964 and became the new nation of Zambia, the injustice was not corrected. And there are still a lot of complaints in the Central Province about the slow pace of development in the area.

The people also complain that they don't get any share of the revenues generated by tourism in the park. The leaders of the Nkoya tribe and some of their people have even demanded the creation of a new province which they want to call Kafue Province. But their demands have fallen on deaf ears, ignored by the national government.

They lost their independence and means of livelihood when the colonial rulers evicted them from their land. And they still have not regained their rights even under their own government, an African government which is predominantly black.

There have been a lot of changes in life in Zambia after the country won independence. One of those changes is the enjoyment of equal rights under the law regardless of race, tribe, religion or or national origin.

But there are some injustices which have not been corrected. The Nkoya case is a good example of that. And there are others, including one involving the eviction of the local people in the area where the Kariba Dam was built on the Zambezi River in the late 1950s.

While the rivers are a major asset to Zambia, their use has had unintended consequences in some cases as we have just seen. But, in general, the benefits far outweigh the disadvantages, although there is an imperative need to corrected the injustices inflicted on some of the indigenous people who were deprived their rights.

Some of the major benefits derived from using rivers such as the Kafue have also trickled down to the grassroots level, for example, in terms of employment for the local people who live along or near these major waterways. The Kafue River is a typical example in this case.

The water from the river is used to irrigate vast expanses of farmland and support other agricultural activities including large estates and sugarcane plantations in the Southern Province.

And besides the Copperbelt Province in the northern part of the country where the Kafue River is an important lifeline to many mining towns and cities, the river also plays a major role in the survival and prosperity of other urban areas such as Kafue – a town located on the northern bank of the river – in Lusaka Province; and Mazabuka, a town which grew around sugarcane plantations in the Southern Province.

But the river also has had environmental problems, mainly pollution, through the years. In the Copperbelt Province in the northern part of the country, the Kafue River has been contaminated by urban waste and discharges from the copper mines in the region.

There has, however, been some improvement as the river continues to flow south. Swampy areas have helped filter the water. These swampy areas have trapped some of the polluted material, acting as a filter and making the river somewhat clean and clearer as it continues to flow south.

There have also been some problems in the area known as the Kafue flats. The Kafue flats are an area of a flat plain through which the river flows as it continues its long journey before it empties into th Zambezi further south and east.

Excessive phosphates discharged from fertiliser used in commercial farming have provided nutrients to algae and other plants, leading to massive growth of weed which has interfered with fish reproduction. The result has been a severe reduction in the population of fish in the river in some of these areas, although fish still remain abundant in the river as a whole.

And in spite of all these problems, the Kafue River is a major source of irrigation for commercial farming in Zambia which in turn provides employment, hence a means of livelihood, for tens of thousands of people in the country.

Commercial plantations especially those bordering the Kafue flats use large quantities of water for irrigation. One of the biggest beneficiaries is the Nakambala Sugar Estate in that area. It uses a lot of water everyday, irrigating the land to grow and sustain sugar cane.

Besides, the Kafue, another major river in the Zambezi basin is the Luangwa. It's one of the four largest rivers in Zambia and plays a major role in supporting large segments of the human population and wildlife.

The Luangwa is also the largest river in the eastern part of Zambia.

But the river's valley has formidable physical barriers which have played a major role in preserving wildlife. The barriers have stopped people from migrating into the area; they would face formidable obstacles if they decided to settle there.

The physical barriers of the valley have also discouraged the construction of roads across the valley. No road crosses the valley. All this has helped to preserve wildlife in the area.

Very few people live in the valley. It's virtually forbidden territory, cordoned off by Mother Nature, especially by physical barriers and abundant wildlife including dangerous ones like elephants and crocodiles which discourage human settlement.

The river itself is home to large populations of dangerous animals, mainly hippos and crocodiles.

One of the main tributaries of the Luangwa is the Lukasashi River. Also known as the Lukusashi, the tributary flows through some of the most important conservation areas in Zambia.

Another important tributary is the Lunsemfwa which merges with the Lukasashi before flowing into the Luangwa River.

Apart from being popular for fishing, the Lukusashi is also a major source of hydroelectricity for the mining city of Kabwe, serving the mines and surrounding areas.

As the Luangwa continues to flow south, where it's identified as the Lower Luangwa, the river finally flows in the Zambezi at the town of Luangwa.

Once known as Feira, the town of Luangwa is the district capital of a district also named Luangwa in the administrative region of Lusaka Province.

Located at the confluence of the Luangwa and Zambezi rivers, what is now known as the town of Luangwa was probably the first European settlement in Zambia.

Around 1720, the Portuguese who colonised neighbouring Mozambique were the first Europeans to establish a settlement at Zumbo on the opposite bank of the Luangwa River in their African colony.

They established the settlement as a trading centre for their commercial activities with members of the Bwila tribe in the area. By 1820, some of the Portuguese had settled in Feira, now Luangwa. The settlement was named Feira by the Portuguese. It's a Portuguese name.

After Zambia won independence from the British colonial rulers in October 1964, the new African government changed the name of the town from Feira to Luangwa.

The town's location is of great strategic significance. It's at a confluence of two major rivers both of which form national boundaries. The Luangwa River is a national boundary separating Zambia from Mozambique; and the

Zambezi forms the border between Zambia and Zimbabwe.

During the liberation struggle in Mozambique and Zimbabwe, the town of Luangwa was a centre of guerrilla activity, used by the African nationalist forces fighting against the colonial rulers. The town was also a focal point during the civil war in Mozambique, serving as a transit point for refugees fleeing from the conflict.

Zambia strongly supported the freedom fighters, triggering reprisals from the white minority regime in Rhodesia, now Zimbabwe, and from the Portuguese colonial forces in Mozambique.

During the liberation and civil wars in the sixties and seventies which devastated Rhodesia and Mozambique, the Great East Road in the eastern part of Zambia which links the Eastern Province with the rest of the country, proved to be highly vulnerable to attack and disruption; being only a few miles from both Mozambique and Zimbabwe. And because of Zambia's support to the freedom fighters, the white minority regimes cut off the road at the Luangwa Bridge. They also destroyed the bridge.

Life in Zambia during the liberation struggle in the countries of southern Africa was profoundly affected in a number of ways. The country as a whole suffered because of economic sanctions imposed on Rhodesia. This meant that Zambia could no longer trade with its white-ruled neighbour. It also meant Zambia goods could no longer go through Rhodesia and through the sea ports in Portuguese-ruled Mozambique.

Life in Zambia, especially in the southern part, was also affected because of security concerns since the country was in a state of war with the countries of southern Africa dominated by white minority regimes.

But all that changed after the countries won freedom and Zambia re-established links with them.

In addition to the Kafue and Luangwa, another river in

the Zambezi basin is the Kabompo. Like the other two rivers, it plays a major role in supporting human and animal life. It's also a very important source of fish, supplementing local diet.

There is also a town named after the Kabompo River. Located in western Zambia, the town of Kabompo was built on the river. It's only a small town but one of historic importance. It was in this town that the colonial authorities kept nationalist leader Kenneth Kaunda from March to July 1959.

The restriction was imposed to prevent him from carrying on his political activities in the quest for independence. And the house in which he stayed during that period is now a national monument.

The Kabompo River finally flows into the Zambezi north of the town of Lukulu. The town is on the Zambezi River. It's a market town and is also located in the Western Province. One of the most important commodities sold in this town and sent to other parts of the country is fish from the Zambezi River.

The other rivers in the Zambezi basin are the Lungwebungu and the Zambezi itself. The Lungwebungu is the largest tributary of the upper Zambezi.

It's a valuable source of fish especially for local people. But it's almost useless as a water highway because of meanders. It's only during the rainy season that it can be used for transport when canoes and small boats are used on the flood.

The biggest and most important river in the Zambezi basin is, of course, the Zambezi itself.

The Zambezi, also spelled Zambesi, is the fourth-longest river in Africa. And among all the rivers on the continent which flow into the Indian Ocean, the Zambezi is the largest.

On its long journey to the Indian Ocean, the Zambezi flows through Angola, then along the borders of four countries – Namibia, Botswana, Zambia and Zimbabwe –

before it enters Mozambique where it empties into the Indian Ocean.

One of the most striking features of the Zambezi River is islands. It has a very large number of islands covered with trees. But the river's most spectacular feature is the Victoria Falls of majestic splendour.

There are other major waterfalls in Zambia, although not as important as the Victoria Falls. They include the Chavuma Falls on the Zambian/Angolan border, and the Ngoye Falls near Sioma in the western part of Zambia.

The Victoria Falls, which are known in one of the local languages as Mosi-oa-Tunya which means "The Mist that Thunders", are located between Zambia and Zimbabwe. They are some of the largest in the world.

The Victoria Falls are considered to be among the Seven Wonders of the World. David Livingstone, the Scottish missionary-doctor and explorer, is believed to have been the first European to see the Victoria Falls.

In Zambia, the falls are officially known as Mosi-oa-Tunya, while in Zimbabwe they're still officially called Victoria Falls.

They're not the highest falls in the world. And they are not the widest. But they are the largest. The falls are 5,600 feet wide and 360 feet high, creating a spectacular sight of falling water.

Victoria Falls is roughly three times the height of North America's Niagara Falls. And it's rivalled only by South America's Iguazu Falls in height and width.

The area of the Victoria Falls is inextricably linked with the history of the Tonga, one of the major ethnic groups in southern Africa found in a number of countries, especially South Africa, Mozambique, Zimbabwe, Malawi and Zambia.

When the southern Tonga people known as the Batoka/Tokalea settled in the area, they called the falls *Shungu na mutitima*. The Ndebele, who came later, named them *aManz' aThunqayo*. And the Batswana and the

Makololo called them *Mosi-oa-Tunya*. All these names mean essentially "the smoke that thunders."

The falls became an increasingly popular attraction during British colonial rule when the British ruled Northern Rhodesia, now Zambia, and South Rhodesia, renamed Zimbabwe. The town of Victoria Falls became the main tourist centre. And it's still an important tourist centre today.

During the liberation wars in the seventies, the number of tourists and other visitors going to see Victoria Falls dropped tremendously, especially on the Rhodesian side. But Zambia was affected as well.

Military reprisals by the white minority regime in Rhodesia against Zambia for its support of the freedom fighters led to the imposition of security measures by the Zambian government including the stationing of soldiers along the border to restrict access to the gorges and some parts of the falls.

When Rhodesia won independence in April 1980 as Zimbabwe, peace and stability to the area returned. The number of tourists also increased, especially in the 1980s and 1990s.

By the end of the 1990s, more than half a million tourists were visiting the area every year. And more visitors were expected.

But not all these visitors are foreigners; not even the majority.

There is a misconception that most tourists who visit Victoria Falls come from Europe and North America as is the case in many other parts of Africa. But that is not the case with Victoria Falls.

Victoria Falls have more Zimbabwean and Zambian visitors than international tourists. The main reason is that it's easy to go to the falls by bus and by train. Therefore, it's not very expensive to go there. You don't need tourist dollars.

Historically, visitors to the Zimbabwean side of the

falls have usually far exceeded those visiting the Zambian side. That's because Zimbabwe is more developed than Zambia, relatively speaking. The people have more money and their country has better facilities. But the political and economic turmoil in Zimbabwe since the late 1990s has had a devastating impact on tourism in that country.

However, the Zambezi River continues to help sustain life on both sides of the border especially in these hard times on the Zimbabwean side. Unfortunately, many lives have also been lost through the years from attacks by crocodiles and hippos found in abundance in this majestic river.

The Zambezi also has a lot of fish. It's also a major source of electricity.

There are two main sources of hydroelectricity on the Zambezi. These are the Kariba Dam which provides hydroelectric power to Zambia and Zimbabwe; and the Cahora Bassa Dam in Mozambique which provides power to both Mozambique and South Africa. There is also a smaller power station at Victoria Falls.

Kariba Dam, which is in Zambia, is a hydroelectric dam in the Kariba Gorge of the Zambezi River basin between Zambia and Zimbabwe. It is one of the largest dams in the world. It's about 1,900 feet long and 420 feet high.

The dam was built by an Italian company between 1955 and 1959. Final construction was completed in1977 after adding another power station. And at least 86 men were killed in accidents when the dam was being built.

Lake Kariba, created by the dam, is 174 miles long.

The creation of the artificial lake forced tens of thousands of the members of the Tonga tribe to leave their traditional homelands to create room for the project. Almost 60,000 people living along the Zambezi in both Zambia and Zimbabwe were forcibly removed.

They were forced to leave their homes and fertile lands that had been used by their ancestors for hundreds of years.

The water reservouir flooded the communities where for centuries the people of the Tonga tribe had farmed, fished, worshipped, raised their children and buried their dead. They were resettled in barren and infertile areas and left to fend for themselves. According to anthropologist Thayer Scudder, who has studied these communities since the late 1950s:

"Today, most are still 'development refugees.' Many live in less-productive, problem-prone areas, some of which have been so seriously degraded within the last generation that they resemble lands on the edge of the Sahara Desert." – (Thayer Scudder, "Pipe Dreams: Can The Zambezi River Supply The Region's Water Needs?" in *Cultural Survival Quarterly*, 31 July 2007).

Little has changed through the years. The Tonga have remained victims of injustice perpetrated by their own national government in the name of modernisation. Where local and national interests clash, the government prevails because national interest is paramount.

Although the dam has indeed been a major asset to Zambia through the years in terms of providing electricity and employment, there is also no question that the project was, from the beginning, a curse to the local people. And it still is one of the most tragic resettlement schemes on the African continent and in the entire world.

In a quest to restore their lives and find justice, the Tonga formed their own advocacy group in 2000 known as the Basilwizi Trust.

The group sees itself as the culmination of numerous efforts by the victims of this injustice who have always wanted to be heard by the government.

In 2005, Basilwizi conducted extensive research on the socio-economic status of the Tonga people and came up with this report:

"The Gwembe Tonga on the Zambian side and the Zimbabwean Tonga are one; but due to separation brought about by the dam, they are now considered different people.

Their languages have become slightly different over the years. Some, especially on the Zimbabwean side, no longer speak Tonga, the language of their ancestors, due to dominance of other indigenous languages."

Basilwizi has also launched initiatives to promote Tonga culture, including preservation of the Tonga language. Efforts include provision of education. and facilities. Other major concerns include food security and access to electricity – still unavailable to the local people more than 50 years after the dam was built.

The group is also calling on the World Bank and other parties involved in building the dam to bring justice to the Tonga. "Calls for reparation, coming many years after the displacement of these people from the land of their ancestors, have not yielded any significant benefits," according to Basilwizi in its recent report, which goes on to state:

"Such compensation could be in monetary terms, decommissioning of the dam, official recognition of past and current injustices suffered, or complete restoration of the ecosystems. A new dialog to correct the wrongs committed should commence.

The Tonga are … trying to find solutions to their predicament and to rise out of the imposed poverty. The perpetrators should not look at this as a social obligation but a realization that this could have been done better...."

Thus, while the members of some ethnic groups have benefited from development projects which have been carried on in their local areas through the years, there are those who have not only benefited; they have also suffered. The Tonga of southern Zambia are a typical example of that. And the lives of tens of thousands of them were changed permanently when the Kariba Dam was built.

On 6 February 2008, BBC reported that heavy rain might lead to flooding, creating a massive outflow of water from Kariba Dam which would force tens of thousands of people downstream to leave their homes and seek refuge elsewhere.

That was in the southeastern part of Zambia, an area that borders Zimbabwe and Mozambique.

The torrential rains which led to flooding also affected Mozambique. According to a report by BBC entitled, "Flood Gates to Open in Mozambique":

"The authorities in Mozambique have begun evacuating thousands more people from the Zambezi river valley.

The move follows an announcement by neighbouring Zambia that it would release water from the Kariba dam.

The water is expected to flow down the Zambezi into areas of Mozambique already struggling to cope with high flood waters. Aid agencies are describing the growing crisis along the Zambezi river valley as going 'from bad to worse.'

Just as the authorities thought the floodwaters had stabilised, the rains have started up once more, says the BBC's Peter Greste. Controllers of the massive dam say they will have to release water or risk having the dam burst in the next week to 10 days.

In Mozambique there are already almost 100,000 evacuees and the reception centres are full to capacity. But with the river already at a record high, they are now looking to move another 40,000 as well as having to re-evacuate people sheltering in centres they thought were safe.

Chris McAiver from the aid organisation Save the Children says the Mozambican authorities have managed the crisis admirably so far, but the pressure from the continuing rainfall is putting immense strain on the already overstretched resources.

Countries across southern Africa - Lesotho, Malawi, Mozambique, Swaziland and Zambia - have been affected by the floods and more people will have to be evacuated.

More rain is forecast to fall this month and it could continue into April, the International Federation of Red Cross and Red Crescent Societies said.

Torrential rains in Zambia and Zimbabwe have swollen the Zambezi river to well above the flood limits. Valleys in Malawi and Mozambique are bearing the brunt as the waters flow down to the Indian Ocean."

Releasing the water from the Kariba Dam is still one of the options the government can still use, although it can also have tragic consequences in terms of lives lost and property destroyed, wreaking havoc in the affected regions.

The name Kariba is thought to be a corruption of the Shona word for a trap. Kariva is a little trap and it's believed that when those who wanted to build the dam tried to explain the nature of the project to the indigenous people, they emphasised that they wanted to build a little trap – hence Kariva – to trap the water.

But the builders of the dam were foreigners and could not pronounce the letter "v" in the word "Kariva." This led to the corruption of the term, replacing "v" with "b" for easy pronunciation, leading to the adoption of the word "Kariba."

In its long course from the northwest where it originates, the Zambezi traverses a vast expanse of territory which includes some of Zambia's most important historical and cultural landmarks. One of the areas of such significance is the residence of the *litunga*, the king of the

41

Lozi or Barotse in western Zambia.

One of the king's capitals, Lealui, is located near the place where the Luanginga River flows into the Zambezi. It's about eight-and-a-half miles west of Mongu, the capital of the Western Province.

Although the Zambezi is one of the major rivers in the world, it's not navigable in most areas. The most navigable part is the lower Zambezi from Cahora Bassa in Mozambique to the Indian Ocean.

As the river gets close to its final destination, the Indian Ocean, it branches out in several parts forming a vast expanse of several branches creating a very large delta. But the size of the delta has been profoundly affected by the construction of two major dams on the Zambezi.

The delta of the Zambezi is today about half as big as it was before the two dams, the Kariba and Cahora Bassa, were built, reducing the outflow.

The Zambezi River is a source of sustenance for millions of people in the region through which it flows for more than 2,000 miles. About 32 million people live in the Zambezi valley, heavily depend on the river for survival.

They're involved in various activities but most of them are engaged in farming and related activities. About 80 per cent of the people who live in the valley depend on agriculture. It is a fertile valley, and the upper river's flood plains are known for their good agricultural land which produces a wide variety of crops including export commodities.

The Zambezi River also is a major source of fish. People who live close to the river catch a lot of fish for their own consumption and for sale. Some people also travel long distances to go and catch some fish from the river.

Local communities sometimes benefit from taxes imposed on outsiders who go to catch some fish from the

Zambezi. A number of towns on roads leading to the river demand 'fish taxes' from outsiders who take the fish to other parts of the country. The fish are considered to be a local resource which should benefit local communities the most; hence the need to impose taxes on outsiders who go in to get some fish.

But the tax is not officially sanctioned by the Zambian government, although high government officials look the other way instead of intervening to stop this activity. And there is no guarantee that the money is spent well by local leaders for the benefit of their communities; it's probably not. It's most likely pocked by the officials themselves who claim to work in the best interest of their local communities.

Besides fish caught for local consumption and for sale to other parts of Zambia, a lot of fish are also caught by people involved in game fishing which takes place in some parts of the river. In fact, fishing is a a very important part of tourism in Zambia and its full potential has not yet been exploited.

Some fish are also sold to other people who are involved in business providing fish as pets. It's a large market with international customers and is regulated by the government and international laws.

The Zambezi River valley is also rich in minerals, although not all of them are being exploited. One of the most important activities in the mineral sector in some parts of the valley is coal mining.

The valley also has fossil fuels. The fuels are another potential source of economic growth in the region and for the country as a whole.

The dams on the Zambezi are also a very important source of income for local people because of the employment opportunities they provide. Employment opportunities include maintenance jobs, with many people working on the dams and at the hydroelectric power stations to make sure they function well.

Many parts of the Zambezi River are major tourist atractions. Victoria Falls alone draws more than 1.5 million people every year. Lake Kariba and Mana Pools also attract large numbers of visitors from different parts of the world and from within Zambia itself.

Mana Pools is an area in the western part of Zimbabwe constituting a national park. It's a region of the lower Zambezi River where the flood plain turns into a vast expanse of temporary lakes at the end of the rainy season. Many animals flock to the area in search of water, making it one of the most popular tourist areas on the entire continent. Tourists from many parts of the world go there to see the animals. It's a spectacular sight.

Although the Zambezi River plays a very important role in the economic wellbeing of the people and the countries of southern Africa, it has never been a major water highway despite its size. It's navigable in some parts. But it has many rapids and has never been used as a means of transport for long distances.

Still, it some times plays an important role in transport. For example, in some parts in the region, it's better to travel by canoe along the river than to use bad roads which are often in very poor condition. The roads are submerged in floods a lot of times. And many small villages along the banks of the Zambezi are accessible only by boat.

The river has also been a victim of pollution through the years. The cities and towns in the region don't have water treatment facilities and release untreated sewage into the river. This causes a lot of problems, spreading diseases such cholera, typhus and dysentery.

Chemicals and other industrial waste discharged into the river also have had a negative impact on the environment. Animals in the river have also been affected in varying degrees. Fish are some of the main victims.

And the construction of two major dams – Kariba and Cahora Bassa – the reduction in the water flow has led to a number of problems. It has affected animals and people in the lower Zambezi region in varying degrees. Some animals have been forced to migrate to other parts. The water reduction has also forced many people to adapt to new ways of life and survival.

Although the Zambezi valley is mostly rural, there are many important towns in the area. It's also not heavily populated but has small populations here and there spread along much of the river's length.

Important towns or urban centres in the valley include Katima Mulilo in Namibia; Mongu, Lukulu, Livingstone, and Sesheke in Zambia; Victoria Falls and Kariba in Zimbabwe; and Songo and Tete in Mozambique.

Although the Zambezi is the main river with important population centres a number of which have developed into towns, some of its major tributaries are also associated with the development of important urban centres; for example, the Kafue on the Copperbelt where the river flows through or near a number of mining towns and cities in that province.

Life in these mining towns is very much at the centre of national life because of the importance of the Copperbelt region as the nation's industrial hub.

But the industrial sector in the country as a whole is very small although it plays an important role in the lives of millions of people in Zambia.

Still, Zambia is an underdeveloped country. And in an underdeveloped country like that where technology does not play a major role in life the way it does in developed nations, survival and development depends on Mother Nature more than anything else. That is why the country is heavily dependent on agriculture. And that is why climate and seasonal changes play a very big role in the lives of millions of people across the country.

In fact, almost the entire the economic, cultural and social life of the country is dominated by seasonal changes. It's a matter of life and death. If there is not enough rain, many people face starvation. But too much rain also causes disaster.

Flooding during the rainy season is common in Zambia, especially in the flood plains, disrupting life including destruction of property as well crops, roads and bridges.

While the rainy season is one of mixed blessings, the dry season also has its advantages and disadvantages.

Bush fires are common during the dry season. The fires are deliberately started by the people in the rural areas for a number of reasons. They do so to flush out animals they want to kill for a meal. They also start fires to clear the land for the next planting season.

But in many cases, the fires are not destructive because there is not much left to burn. Such fires are an annual occurrence, making it impossible for large quantities of dry material – such as grass – that can be burnt to pile up. But they do sometimes kill animals and destroy crops especially when the rains end early and when fires are started before crops are harvested.

Although the fires can destroy almost everything they touch, there are plant which they can not completely destroy. There also fire-resistant plants in Zambia. The presence of these plants shows that such fires – used to clear the land – have been an integral part of life in traditional communities across the country for centuries.

The use of such fires is an integral part of the traditional practice of farming known as *chitemene*.

Chitemene, also spelled as *sitememe*, is a word from the Bemba language – one of the main languages spoken in Zambia – which means a "place where branches have been cut for a garden."

The term *chitemene* is used in a larger context to describe a traditional system of slash-and-burn farming practised in different parts of the country. It's commonly used in Northwestern, Copperbelt, Central, Northern, and Luapula provinces.

All those provinces are in the northern part of Zambia

where the Bemba and members of related tribes are dominant.

Crops planted in the burned area include maize, cassava, millet and sorghum. And they're all dependent on rain. There are no irrigation canals to sustain them.

The ability to grow enough food during the rainy season which will enable the people to survive during the long dry season is also a major factor in population growth and distribution throughout Zambia.

Seasons regulate almost everything. Even prayers are offered, invoking the power of the ancestors to intercede with the Almighty on behalf of the living. The people pray for rain and for plentiful harvest. They also pray for abundant meat.

In many fundamental respects, life in Zambia is typical of life in other countries across the continent whose level of development is not much different from Zambia's.

Traditionally, members of some tribes in Zambia – as well as in many other parts of Africa – divide their activities based on seasonal changes.

They grow crops during the rainy season. And they fish and hunt during the dry season when animals are easily found near rivers and lakes, drinking water, making it easy for the people to kill them for meat. The people also start fires during the dry season to flush out animals they want to catch. The animals also run into traps when they try to escape the fires.

Although Zambia has a moderate climate, without extremes in temperature, it's considered to be vulnerable to climate change which might lead to differences in amounts of rainfall. The changes may also reduce the length of the rainy season.

Such changes will have profound impact on the lives of the people and the wellbeing of the nation as a whole because it's mostly an agricultural country.

The vast majority of the people earning a living from subsistence farming. Few have large farms like many farmers, especially whites, do in neighbouring Zimbabwe. But the country also has significant quantities of minerals which have not been fully exploited.

There was a time when copper was king. It was the biggest foreign exchange earner for many years; and it still is even today. But it has lost much of its value through the decades, although it still remains a very important export commodity and source of employment.

Other major minerals are cobalt, zinc, lead, coal, gold, silver, and uranium. Zambia also has a lot of hydroelectric potential, with most of the electricity being generated by the Zambezi River.

Although Zambia is potentially rich in terms of farmland, minerals, tourism and other resources, poverty remains a major problem across the country. About 70 per cent of Zambians live below the poverty line.

In the rural areas, the percentage of those who live below the poverty line is higher. Almost 80 per cent of them do.

The number of Zambians who live below the poverty line is lowest in towns and cities. About 53 per cent of Zambians in urban areas live below the poverty line.

Deforestation, soil erosion and desertification are also major problems in Zambia.

Zambia's economic performance has not been very good through the decades since independence in 1964. When the country won independence, it was one of the richest in Africa. In fact, Zambia's per capita income was higher than South Korea's.

Today, South Korea's per capita income is much higher than Zambia's. South Korea's per capita income was about $28,000 in 2008, and Zambia's, only about $400. It's a glaring contrast in the economic performance between the two countries.

But such dismal performance is not peculiar to Zambia. It's a continental phenomenon. As one African writer, Godfrey Mwakikagile, who comes from Tanzania – his home region, Mbeya, in the Southern Highlands in southwestern Tanzania borders Zambia – states in his book, *Africa is in A Mess: What Went Wrong and What Should Be Done*:

"Since independence in the sixties, Africa has performed poorly in most areas because of bad leadership and bad policies, not because of weak genes.

Most countries on the continent won independence by 1968. Yet, an entire generation later, they have little to show for all those years they have ruled themselves.

No one expects a country to develop in 30 or 40 years. But no one expects it to do nothing either. There is no excuse for the kind of economic retardation that has taken place in most countries across Africa since independence. A generation is not a week. When compared with other parts of the developing world, Africa has performed miserably in every conceivable way. And statistics tell the story, a sad story.

In 1965, Nigeria was richer than Indonesia, and Ghana richer than Thailand. Today Indonesia is three times richer than Nigeria, and Thailand five times richer than Ghana.

In 1965, Uganda was richer than South Korea. And in 1967, Zambia also was richer than South Korea. Zambia had a per capita income of $200, and South Korea, $120. After 30 years, South Korea's gross domestic product per person was more than $10,000 in 1998, and Zambia's $400.[4]

Yet, by African standards, Zambia is considered to be one of the richest countries on the continent in spite of all the misery, hunger and starvation ravaging this country endowed with abundant minerals and arable land more than enough to feed its entire population.

And all African countries combined have a smaller gross domestic product than that of Belgium, a country of only 10 million people, and one of the smallest in the world. By contrast, Africa's population is more than 700 million on a continent endowed with abundant natural resources.

The gross domestic product of African countries is not only smaller but a mere fraction of Belgium's. What is even more depressing is that Indonesia, a developing country which in 1965 was poorer than Nigeria, has a bigger gross domestic product than that of all the black African countries combined. Yet, Indonesia itself was a colony like the African countries and won independence roughly around the same time that African countries did during the post-World War II era.

It is just as sad, probably even more so, when we look at the dismal performance of black Africa from another perspective.

There are 40 black African countries out of 53 on the entire continent which includes the island nations of Madagascar, Mauritius, the Comoros, and the Seychelles, all on the Indian Ocean; Cape Verde, and Sao Tome & Principe on the Atlantic.

More than half of the gross domestic product of the black African countries is contributed by only two countries: South Africa and Nigeria. That means a total of 38 black African countries – almost the entire sub-Saharan region - have a combined gross domestic product which is only about a third of Indonesia's.

And the devastating impact of AIDS, civil wars and corruption makes things worse, much worse, with no relief in sight. Now, an increasing number of people across Africa are turning to churches calling for divine intervention to alleviate their plight.

Something is wrong, terribly wrong. But unlike in the past when it was fashionable for many Africans to blame colonialism and imperialism for almost all the problems our countries faced after we won independence, an increasing number of them today, especially those of the younger generation, insist on accountability within Africa itself as they apportion guilt accordingly; instead of

– underdevelopment
reasons: bad leadership / AIDs / decrease of
copper prices

blaming colonialists and imperialists for the perpetual misery - thanks to tyranny, corruption, poverty and disease - hundreds of millions of Africans have to endure all their lives.

To these millions, independence has remained an abstract ideal without any concrete benefits in their lives as they remain trapped in poverty and continue to be ravaged by disease while billions of dollars in foreign aid and taxes paid by the toiling masses are being stolen and squandered by unscrupulous politicians and bureaucrats together with their cronies and mistresses. It is clear where the problem lies. It lies within, not without." – (Godfrey Mwakikagile, *Africa is in A Mess: What Went Wrong and What Should Be Done*, New Africa Press, 2006, pp. 12 – 14).

Zambia's per capita income is about one-half of what it was at independence in 1964 and has earned the country the unenviable distinction as one of the poorest in the entire world.

Compounding the problem is the fact that population growth outstrips economic growth, thus perpetuating poverty. And the devastating impact of the AIDS pandemic has made things worse. AIDS has killed a very large number of the most active members of the labour force and it continues to do so.

Also, the country's economic policies pursued along socialist lines since independence failed to fuel economic growth through the decades. The situation got worse when copper prices fell sharply in the 1970s, seriously damaging the economy of a country that almost solely depended on copper.

The decline of the copper industry continued for decades And it has not fully recovered, although there has been some improvement in the copper market since 2002, leading to an increase in revenues and foreign exchange earnings.

agriculture
85% of total employment

The government is also trying to diversify the economy and reduce its heavy dependence on a single commodity, copper, as the engine of progress. Agriculture, tourism and gemstone mining are expected to contribute substantially to the nation's economic growth.

Other minerals such as nickel, tin and uranium, besides copper, offer bright prospects for the country. And it's expected that nickel will take over from copper as the country's main export among minerals.

Zambia also has significant amounts of other minerals in commercial quantities which have not been fully exploited. They include cobalt, zinc, lead, emeralds, gold, and silver.

Although Zambia is one of the most urbanised countries in Africa, the urban population – about an entire half of the nation's total population – is concentrated in a few urban zones strung along the major transport corridors. That's in sharp contrast with the rural areas which have a low population density.

Zambia is also one of the few countries south of the Sahara whose unemployment problem is compounded by the fact that an entire half of its population is urban; thus, almost totally dependent on a wage economy since people who live in towns and cities can not be self-sufficient the way their counterparts are in the rural areas where people grow their own food and live in their own houses or huts – without buying food and paying rent.

But it is agriculture which remains the backbone of the economy. It accounts for 85 per cent of total employment, formal and informal, thus eclipsing the other sectors of the economy.

The main cash crop is maize. It's also Zambia's staple food in the urban and rural areas.

In addition to maize, sorghum and cassava, other important crops include soybeans, sugar cane, sunflower, wheat, cotton, tobacco, and a variety of fruits and vegetables.

52

Another important agricultural sector is floriculture. It's a growing field and it's expected to contribute significantly to the nation's economic wellbeing. In fact, agricultural non-traditional exports – including flowers – now rival the mining industry in foreign exchange earnings.

The country also has bright prospects in terms of agricultural output because all of its arable land is not used. Less than 20 per cent of Zambia's arable land is used for growing crops and for the production of other agricultural commodities; which means there is plenty of land left for expansion of the agricultural sector.

Unfortunately, the agricultural sector has suffered through the years from low prices for commodities, shortage of high-skilled manpower and lack of investments, among other problems. And all these problems continue to impede progress in one of Africa's potentially richest countries.

But prospects are bright because the country can not afford to ignore agriculture which constitutes the back bone of its economy. Agriculture also is the major means of livelihood for the vast majority of Zambians whose lives and destiny are inextricably tied to land.

That's the only life insurance they have. Almost everything they do has to do with land.

Even the country's struggle for independence was based on land. The people fought to get their land back. There is no independence without land.

Land also has spiritual significance in the lives of Africans as their ancestral home and as the dwelling place of their departed ancestors.

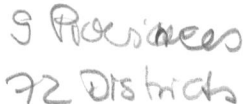

9 Provinces
72 Districts

Part Three:

Provinces

ZAMBIA is divided into nine administrative regions called provinces. Each province is subdivided into districts. There are 72 districts.

The provinces are Central Province, Copperbelt, Eastern, Luapula, Lusaka, Northern, North-Western, Southern, and Western Province.

Central Province

More than any other province, the Central Province is closely identified with the history and identity of Zambia as a nation because it's considered to be the birthplace of the independence movement. It's where the party which led the country to independence was founded.

The party was the United National Independence Party (UNIP). It was founded in Kabwe which is also the capital of the Central Province. The party was led by Kenneth Kaunda. He became Zambia's first president and led the country for 27 years from 1964 to 1991 when he lost the presidential election to union leader Frederick Chiluba after the introduction of multi-party democracy.

The Central Province is also home to Mulungushi. Mulungushi is the name of a river – and a small town nearby – which has taken on a symbolic and historical meaning synonymous with the independence and identity of the nation, and has been given to a number of events, localities, buildings and organisations in the country. For example, there is the Mulungushi Declaration, a policy statement made by President Kenneth Kaunda in 1968 on the nationalisation of the major means of production to transform the country into a socialist nation.

There is also Mulungushi Hall in the nation's capital, Lusaka. It's an international conference and convention centre used as an official venue by the Zambian government.

Mulungushi Hall was also the site of several conferences and negotiations of the anti-apartheid and independence movements of the countries of southern Africa during the sixties, seventies, eighties and nineties.

Then there is Mulungushi House, a large office building in Lusaka which is home to government departments and businesses; Mulungushi Village, a suburb of Lusaka; Mulungushi College in Kabwe; a number of roads and businesses named Mulungushi – such as the Zambia-China Mulungushi Textiles Ltd.; Mulungushi Dam on the Mulungushi River, and other Mulungushis in other parts of the country.

They all remind one of the Central Province where the name, Mulungushi, originated.

And it all started with the struggle for independence.

In 1960 in what was then known as Northern Rhodesia, now Zambia, African nationalists who had broken away from the African National Congress (of

Northern Rhodesia) wanted to convene a conference under the banner of a new party, the United National Independence Party (UNIP) on how to pursue the independence struggle. They wanted to hold the conference in a place where they would not be under the watchful eye of the colonial authorities.

A site was chosen on a rocky area by the Mulungushi River north of Broken Hill – a town that was renamed Kabwe after independence – where up to 2,000 participants could meet in the open air and camp in temporary shelters and in an area where there was a good supply of water.

The conference led to UNIP – under the leadership of Kenneth Kaunda – becoming the major party in the struggle for independence. After that, the area – which came to be known as Mulungushi Rock – was used for UNIP party conferences and for major policy speeches such as the Mulungushi Declaration or Mulungushi Reforms in 1968.

Later, it came to be known as the "Mulungushi Rock of Authority"and has been used by other political parties for their party conferences and major speeches.

All this has given the Central Province a unique place in Zambia's political history. The province has, literally – not only geographically – been central to the evolution of Zambian political politics and other major developments of national significance.

There are six districts in the province: Chibombo, Kabwe, Kapiri Mposhi, Mkushi, Mumbwa, and Serenje.

Chibombo District is located between the Lukanga Swamp in the west and the end of the Luangwa valley in the east. It includes good commercial farmland north of the nation's capital Lusaka.

The district capital is also named Chibombo. The town is on the Great North Road and is near the Lukanga Swamp.

The Lukanga Swamp has many islands. There are

several inhabited islands which stay dry through the rainy season. The swamp also has floating islands of papyrus which are used by fishermen as temporary fishing camps.

The Lukanga Swamp occupies a geographically central location for the country as a whole.

But, despite its central location, the Lukanga Swamp remains relatively inaccessible. Even government officials, local and national, don't pay much attention to the area. But they would have if it was a major tourist attraction, bringing money into the country.

Local people who live in villages in the area do a lot of fishing in the swamp, using traditional methods. Some of the fish caught are sold to other people in Zambia, mainly urban residents in Lusaka and Kabwe, and to others in the Copperbelt, the mining area around the urban centres of Ndola, Kitwe, Chingola, Luanshya and Mufulira.

But there has been a decline in the number of fish caught in the Lukanga Swamp because of over-fishing.

Besides fishing, the people in the area also farm and grow crops on the edge of the floodplain.

The Lukanga Swamp is also home to a wide variety of wild life including hippos, crocodiles, and pythons. And the western side of the swamp has elephants, buffaloes and antelopes among other animals.

The area may be a haven for animals but it's also a kind of trap for them. Poachers have killed and continue to kill many animals and poaching is now a serious problem.

There are other problems in the area including deforestation.

Deforestation for charcoal production and for slash-and-burn farming constitutes a major threat to the Lukanga Swamp ecosystem. resulting in soil erosion, turbidity of water and siltation.

In nearly all areas northeast of the swamp forests have been cleared especially for charcoal production, and land clearing for farming has been extensive on the northeast, east and southern sides of the swamp. Only the western side remains relatively untouched.

Game parks are another important feature of Central Province.

Kabwe is another district in the Central Province. The provincial capital, Kabwe, is also the district capital or headquarters of Kabwe District.

Kapiri Mposhi is another district in the Central Province whose name is also shared by the district headquarters.

The town of Kapiri Mposhi also occupies a special place in the history of Zambia during the post-colonial era and that of the liberation struggle in southern Africa.

It's the eastern terminal of the Tanzania-Zambia Railway, officially known as the Tanzania-Zambia Railway Authority or TAZARA. The terminal is at New Kapiri Mposhi. The railway was built by the Chinese partly to reduce Zambia's dependence on the white-ruled countries of southern Africa as an outlet to the sea for its exports and imports.

Zambia, like Tanzania, was deeply involved in the liberation struggle in southern Africa and was therefore in a state of war with the white minority regimes in the region.

Zambia also severed ties with those regimes and turned east, to Tanzania, for an outlet to the sea. Completion of the Tanzania-Zambia Railway was the culmination of this dream, with Kapiri Mposhi being one of the most important stations on this transnational railway which was completed in 1976.

Another district in the Central Province is Mkushi whose capital is also known as Mkushi.

The town of Mkushi is also well-known for its commercial farms.

Mumbwa District is another administrative constituency of the Central Province. Its capital is Mumbwa located on the Great West Road.

The Great West Road runs from the nation's capital

Lusaka to Mongu, the capital of the Western Province, and connects the Western Province to the rest of the country. It also serves as the main highway of the western half of the Central Province.

The Great West Road is the only main road that goes through Mumbwa District. The district covers the western part of the Central Province.

Mumbwa District is also known for its production of cotton.

The main tribes in Mumbwa District are the Ila in the southern and southeastern part of the district; the Kaonde in the northern part; and the Lenje in the northeast in the area bordering Kabwe District.

There are also significant numbers of people of different tribes from the west and northwest. They include the Lozi and the Nkoya from the western and central-western parts of Zambia; the Luvale (or Lovale) from the northwestern area of the country; and the Shona from what was then Southern Rhodesia.

The Shona fled from conflicts in their homeland and settled in the southern part of Zambia where they became integrated with members of the Tonga tribe in that part of the country.

Mumbwa District was also once a site for mineral prospectors. And small-scale mines once operated there. They were mostly copper and gold mines. But most of them are now closed. But the gold mine at Luiri, also once closed, is now back in operation.

Another district in the Central Province is Serenje. The district's capital is also named Serenje.

Serenje District is inhabited by members of the Lala tribe.

Like most languages spoken in the Copperbelt and Central provinces, the language of the Lala people, which is also known as Lala, is a dialect of the Bemba language. And like most ethnic groups in the central, northern and northwestern parts of Zambia, the Lala are said to have migrated from the Luba-Lunda kingdom in what is now the Democratic Republic of Congo (DRC).

Therefore they are Luba and Lunda in terms of origin. The Luba and the Lunda are some of the largest ethnic groups in Congo and in Central Africa.

The overwhelming majority of the people in Serenje district are peasants. They consume most of what they produce and use rudimentary techniques of subsistence farming like the rest of their fellow countrymen living the traditional way of life in the rural areas in other parts of Zambia.

The district is well-endowed in terms of agricultural potential. It has rich soil, luxuriant vegetation and thick forests. But all this potential has not been fully exploited to develop the area.

When the country was under British colonial rule as Northern Rhodesia, the colonial rulers designated Serenje as a *boma*.

In the Swahili language, there is a word, *boma*, which means "fort" or "fortress." It usually refers to colonial outposts established by the colonial rulers in different parts of Africa to facilitate imperial rule; not much different in terms of function from the *boma* in Serenje and other parts of what was then Northern Rhodesia.

After the Central Province, we are going to look at the Copperbelt Province which is often referred to simply as the Copperbelt.

Copperbelt Province

The Copperbelt Province covers the mineral-rich Copperbelt region. The province also has farming and bush areas in its southern part.

The Copperbelt was the backbone of the country's economy during colonial rule. And it offered bright prospects for newly-independent Zambia.

The new government hoped and expected that it would fuel economic growth. And for a while, it did sustain the economy and provide prosperity.

But the region's economic importance declined years later, especially in 1973 when there was a sharp drop in copper prices worldwide. The role copper played in Zambia's economic growth was further compromised when the government pursued economic policies which harmed the copper industry.

The Copperbelt Province borders Katanga Province – in the Democratic Republic of Congo – which is also rich in minerals. The two regions have similar and sometimes identical geological features which are responsible for the abundance of minerals in that part of Africa.

The Copperbelt Province has some of the largest and most important towns and cities in Zambia: Ndola and Kitwe which are the second- and third-largest, respectively; Chingola, fifth-largest; Mufulira, sixth-largest; Luanshya, seventh-largest; and Chililabombwe, formerly known as Bancroft during colonial rule, whose main economic activity is copper mining like that of the other towns and cities on the Copperbelt.

The Copperbelt Province is the economic hub of Zambia. It's also the most urbanised and most industrialised among all the provinces.

The province has no national parks. But it has two wildlife sanctuaries.

The Copperbelt Province is divided into 10 districts: Chililabombwe, Chingola, Kalulushi, Kitwe, Luanshya, Lufwanyama, Masaiti, Mpongwe, Mufulira, and Ndola.

Chingola, Kitwe, Luanshya, Mufulira and Ndola will be addressed in the next part of the book dealing with major towns and cities. The focus here is on Kalulushi and Lufwanyama.

Kalulushi District is predominantly agricultural like most parts of Zambia. Its capital is also named Kalulushi.

The town of Kalulushi was established in 1953 as a

company town for workers at the nearby Chibuluma copper and cobalt mine. It became a public town in 1958.

The town of Kalulushi is located 9 miles west of Kitwe which is also the nearest railway station. The town's major employer is the Zambia Consolidated Copper Mines (ZCCM).

The Chati Forest Reserve west of the town of Kalulushi has large plantations of eucalyptus, tropical pine, and other exotic tree species which are a source of wood supply for the mining industry. The Zambian Electricity Supply Company (ZESCO), which is the main provider of electricity in the country, is also a major consumer of the wood products from the Chati Forest Reserve.

Another district in the Copperbelt Province is Lufwanyama whose destiny is also inextricably linked with that of its headquarters or capital. The district's capital is also called Lufwanyama.

Lufwanyama is a small town. And although it's not very far from the mining cities of the Copperbelt which collectively constitute the most developed part of Zambia, it has not benefited from the relative prosperity of these urban centres. It does not even have electricity. And there is no hospital in town.

It's only 37 miles from the urban centres in the Copperbelt which are located east of this small town. And the magnetic pull of these cities on Lufwanyama is obvious even if it's not beneficial to the town.

The town is not even on the map of Zambia. But it's located near the Lufwanyama River after which it's named.

The river flows from north to south about 40 miles west of the city of Kitwe and empties into the Kafue River which is the most central and most urban of the Zambian rivers. The Kafue is also the longest and largest among the rivers which flow only within Zambia without crossing national boundaries or originating in neighbouring countries.

Conflict with
Malawi 68 our
Eastern Province

Next we look at the Eastern Province.

Eastern Province

The Eastern Province has some of the best tourist sites in Zambia.

The Luangwa valley is in this province. The valley has some of the best wildlife areas in Africa.

The Eastern Province also has the unenviable distinction of being the only province in Zambia which was claimed by another country.

During the reign of Malawi's president, Dr. Hastings Kamuzu Banda, relations between Zambia and Malawi deteriorated for a number of reasons including Banda's willingness to cooperate and establish diplomatic relations with apartheid South Africa in defiance of the wishes of the other member states of the Organisation of African Unity (OAU) which passed a resolution against that.

Dr. Banda also claimed the entire Eastern Province of Zambia as part of Malawi, prompting Zambian President Kenneth Kaunda to tell Banda to go ahead and declare war on Zambia. According to *Africa Contemporary Record: Annual Survey and Documents 1968 – 1969*:

"(As with Rhodesia), Zambia's relations with another neighbour, Malawi, deteriorated in September (1968) following a claim by President Banda to four districts in Tanzania and Zambia.

Dr. Banda reportedly claimed that 'the real boundary' between Malawi and Zambia should be the Luangwa River embracing the whole of Zambia's Eastern Province. President Kaunda challenged Dr. Banda 'to go ahead and declare war on Zambia.'

Zambia would not establish diplomatic relations with Malawi, he said, until Dr. Banda had renounced his claims to Zambian territory." – Colin Legum and John Drysdale, editors, *Africa Contemporary Record: Annual Survey and Documents 1968 – 1969*, London: Africa Research, Limited, 1969, pp. 250, and 180; *Times of Zambia*, Ndola, Zambia, 12 December 1968).

The territorial dispute with Tanzania also had to do with Lake Nyasa whose name Dr. Banda changed to Lake Malawi claiming the lake belonged exclusively to Malawi and was not shared with Tanzania:

"A Tanzanian note in January, 1967, objected to maps which showed the Malawian-Tanzanian boundary as running along the eastern and northern shores of Lake Nyasa.

Tanzania contended the boundary passes through the middle of the lake and that the change was made illegally by the British government on the declaration of the Rhodesian Federation (in 1953).

Dr. Banda counter-claimed that the lake had always belonged to Malawi, and that he had every right to change its name to Lake Malawi....By September 1968, Dr. Banda...laid further claim to four districts in Tanzania....

Speaking at the Malawi Congress Party's annual convention on September 17, Dr. Banda...announced he was he was putting the first of many gunboats on Lake Nyasa to start patrols as an answer to Tanzania's 'claim.' Dr. Nyerere described these claims as as 'expansionist outbursts which do not scare us, and do not deserve my reply'....

Malawi's territorial claims to districts in Tanzania provoked President Nyerere to retort that Dr. Banda was 'insane'; but, he warned, 'Dr. Banda must not be ignored; the powers behind him are not insane.'" – (*Africa Contemporary Record*, ibid., pp. 180, and 220).

A few years earlier, Dr. Banda also claimed parts of

Mozambique. He was then the leader of the independence movement in Nyasaland and was on his way to becoming the first president of his country which was renamed Malawi after independence.

Dr. Banda went to see Nyerere and encouraged him also to claim a chunk of Mozambican territory. As Nyerere explained in one of his last speeches on 15 December 1997 at an international conference at the University of Dar es Salaam, Tanzania, not long before he died about two years later:

"In 1961 we became independent. In 1962, early 1962, I resigned as prime minister and then a few weeks later I received Dr. Banda. *Mungu amuweke mahali pema* (May God rest his soul in peace). I received Dr. Banda. We had just, FRELIMO had just been established here and we were now in the process of starting the armed struggle.

So Banda comes to me with a big old book, with lots and lots of maps in it, and tells me, 'Mwalimu, what is this, what is Mozambique? There is no such thing as Mozambique.' I said, 'What do you mean there is no such thing as Mozambique?'

So he showed me this map, and he said: 'That part is part of Nyasaland. That part is part of Southern Rhodesia, that part is Swaziland, and this part, which is the northern part, Makonde part, that is *your* part.'

So Banda disposed of Mozambique just like that. I ridiculed the idea, and Banda never liked anybody to ridicule his ideas. So he left and went to Lisbon to talk to Salazar about this wonderful idea. I don't know what Salazar told him. That was '62." – (Godfrey Mwakikagile, *Nyerere and Africa: End of an Era*, Dar es Salaam, Tanzania: New Africa Press, Fifth Edition, February 2010, pp. 554 - 555).

But Banda did not pursue his expansionist ambitions any further beyond rhetoric. Tanzania kept its territory, as did Mozambique, although the dispute with Tanzania over Lake Nyasa continues today. And the Eastern Province of Zambia remained an integral part of Zambia.

The province has 8 districts: Chadiza, Chama, Chipata, Katete, Lundazi, Mambwe, Nyimba, and Petauke.

The district headquarters have the same names as the districts just as the rest do in all the other provinces.

Chadiza is the capital of Chadiza District.

The district lies in the extreme southeastern corner of Zambia bordering Malawi to its east and Mozambique to its south.

Another district in the Eastern Province is Chama. Its capital is also called Chama.

It's one of the most remote district headquarters in the country. It lies just inside the eastern edge of the upper Luangwa Rift Valley at the foot of the highlands dividing Zambia and Malawi.

The town has only one gravel road.

There are no roads west from Chama across the Luangwa valley. But there is a small road which runs along Zambia's border with Malawi going north before crossing into Isoka District in the Northern Province west of the Nyika Plateau.

The Nyika Plateau is in northern Malawi. A small portion of the plateau is in northeastern Zambia. It towers above Lake Nyasa, so-called Lake Malawi, a name used mostly in Malawi but which is not accepted by Tanzania which also shares the lake.

The capital of the Eastern Province, Chipata, is also the headquarters of Chipata District.

We look at Luapula Province next.

Luapula Province

Luapula Province is located in the northern part of the country. It's one of Zambia's provinces which border the

Democratic Republic of Congo (DRC). And it's named after Luapula River.

The provincial capital is Mansa. It's also the headquarters of Mansa District.

Luapula Province extends from Lake Bangweulu to Lake Mweru and includes parts of the two lakes and some of the islands in those lakes. The province is home to the members of the Bemba ethnic group who also live in other provinces mainly in northern Zambia.

The Bemba are the largest and dominant ethnic group in Zambia. And their language, Bemba, is the most widely used indigenous language in the country; virtually a lingua franca.

Other ethnic groups in Luapula Province include the Lunda who straddle the Zambian/Congolese border; the Kabende, Aushi, and Chishinga.

Major economic activities in Luapula Province include farming and fishing.

The main road in the province is the Samfya-Mansa-Mwansambowe-Nchelenge highway. The highway is also informally known as the Zambia Way.

Luapula Province covers the northern and eastern banks of the Luapula River.

During the 1800s, the valley of this river was dominated by the Lunda kingdom of Mwata Kazembe.

Known by the title 'Mwata' or 'Mulopwe' which is equivalent to 'Paramount Chief', the ruler of this traditional homeland is a highly important political figure in the traditional context. And the *mutomboko* festival held annually in the Luapula valley and Lake Mweru area by the people who inhabit this kingdom or chieftainship stands out as one of the most important traditional festivals in Zambia.

The *mutomboko* ceremony is the second-largest of its kind aimed at preserving and promoting indigenous cultures in the country. It's held at the end of July and attracts about 20,000 people including the president of

Zambia.

Drawing on previous ceremonies and traditions, it includes dances symbolising the migration of the Luba-Lunda and the conquest of the Luapula valley by the first chiefs in an area that now largely constitutes Luapula Province.

The province is bordered along the Luapula River, through Lake Mweru and to its north, by Katanga Province in Congo; a territorial arrangement which at times has led to disputes and conflict.

The Congo Pedicle, which is part of Katanga Province, divides Zambia. It protrudes between Luapula Province and the industrial and commercial heartland of the Copperbelt, causing logistical problems which have been partly resolved by the construction of the Luapula Bridge and the Samfya-Serene road.

The problems have also been further alleviated by the construction of the Chembe Bridge.

The Congo Pedicle – in French known as *la botte du Katanga*, meaning *Katanga boot* – refers to the southeastern salient of Katanga Province which sticks into Zambia, almost dividing it into two lobes like the wings of a butterfly. The term "Pedicle" is used in the sense of "a little foot." "Congo Pedicle" is also used to refer to the Congo Pedicle road which crosses it.

The creation of the Congo Pedicle and the way the territorial boundaries were drawn is an example of the total disregard of African interests by the imperial powers who partitioned the continent at the Berlin Conference of 1885 during the Scramble for Africa.

Efforts have been made to connect the two parts of Zambia separated by this intrusion. But much work remains to be done.

Luapula Province's infrastructural problems remain a major obstacle to economic development. And what's called Luapula's provincial highway, also known as the Zambia Way – running from Samfya to Mansa,

Mwansabombwe and Nchelege – is not very much of a highway.

Besides, Samfya, Mansa, and Nchelege all of which are district capitals, Mwansabombwe is also an important town in its own way even if it's not one of the district capitals in Luapula Province.

Located on the border with Congo, Mwansabombwe is also known as Kazembe.

Kazembe, or Kasembe, is the name used for Mwata Kazembe's town, especially on maps and by the Zambia postal service. But the correct name for the town is Mwansabombwe which means "where Mwansa works."

The second half of the name, "bombwe," is almost identical to a term in my native language of Nyakyusa spoken by the Nyakyusa people across the border in southwestern Tanzania, also in northern Malawi, and by the many Nyakyusa immigrants who have lived in Zambia for decades since colonial times when they migrated to what was then Northern Rhodesia to work in the mines. The vast majority of them settled on the Copperbelt.

In Nyakyusa language, known as Kinyakyusa, or *ikiNyakyusa* in our language, *mbombo* or *imbombo* means "work." *Ukubomba imbombo* means "to work." *Ngubomba imbombo* means "I work." The term is very similar to *bombwe* in the town's name *Mwansabombwe* – meaning "where it works" – in Luapula Province.

The similarity is a defining feature of Bantu languages because they are related, showing a common origin of the people who speak them, although there is no Bantu race.

The Bemba and the Luba who live in that town and in Luapula Province as well as in other parts of Zambia call the town Mwansabombwe.

In English, the town is known as Kazembe Village or simply Kazembe since, traditionally, a settlement is sometimes named after a chief or a headman of the area rather than the location.

The Luba-Lunda shared with many tribes the custom,

now discontinued, of moving to another village or a new site on the death of the chief. Therefore, historical references to a village or a town may actually be to a different location. For instance, when the explorer David Livingstone visited Mwata Kazembe in 1867 and 1868, what he identified as "Casembe's town" in his writings was further north at a place where there is now a town called Kanyembo.

David Livingstone's description of the area is contained in David Livingstone & Horace Waller, ed., *The Last Journals of David Livingstone in Central Africa from 1865 to his Death, Two Volumes*, published by John Murray in 1874.

In the past, the incumbent chief was promoted to Mwata (paramount chief), and Kanyembo was the site of Mwata Kazembe's capital when it was visited by David Livingstone in 1867.

Kanyembo is located on the tarred road known as the Zambia Way which is also the main road in Luapula Province.

The main economic activity in Kanyembo is fishing while farming is the main occupation in the hinterland areas around this settlement.

In addition to large mango trees typical of traditional villages in northern Zambia, a notable feature of the Kanyembo area is the existence of mature oil palms which are not native to this part of Zambia and do not grow naturally anywhere else in the country. But they are native to the Lunda kingdom 186 miles west from where the Lunda-Kazembe migrated. However, there is no historical record explaining how and when the oil palms were taken to the Kanyembo area.

The town, or village, of Mwansabombwe is located at a place where the Ngona River flows into the swamps of the Luapula River south of Lake Mweru. A number of channels through the swamps and lagoons facilitate fishing as well as trade with the people across the border in Katanga Province in the Democratic Republic of Congo (DRC). The trade is mostly illegal.

The town is close to the middle point of the tarred road informally known as the "Valley Road."

All those features and the town's status since the 1890s as Mwata Kazembe's capital make Mwansabombwe one of the largest centres of trade, population and culture in the Luapula valley with an estimated population of 50,000.

And it retains its rural and traditional African character relatively unspoiled by foreign intrusion during the colonial era, earning it distinction as the "largest village in central Africa." It's also the pride of Luapula Province.

Luapula Province also has a number of areas which serve as sanctuaries for wildlife.

Luapula Province is divided into 7 districts: Chienge, Kawambwa, Mansa, Milenge. Mwense, Nchelenge, and Samfya.

The capital of Chienge District is Chienge.

During colonial times, Chienge was a *boma*. A *boma* is a livestock enclosure, a stockade or kind of fort, or a district government office.

The term *boma* is used in many parts of eastern, central and southern Africa and is incorporated into many African languages as well as colonial varieties of English, French and German.

As a livestock enclosure, *boma* is the equivalent of "kraal." The term *boma* is used in areas influenced by Swahili and the latter in areas influenced by Afrikaans.

In the form of fortified villages or camps, *bomas* were commonplace in east-central Africa in the 1700s and 1800s in areas affected by the slave trade, tribal wars and colonial conquest, and were built by both sides in such conflicts.

In British colonies, especially in remote areas, *boma* came to be used to mean colonial government offices because in the late 1800s, such offices usually included a fortified police station or military barracks, often in the form of a timber stockade, though some had stone walls. Many were called forts; for example Fort Hall in Uganda; Fort Jameson in what is now the Eastern Province in southeastern Zambia; and Fort Elwes in Zambia's Central Province.

In the 20th century, the term *boma* came to mean the district or provincial government headquarters even where fortifications were no longer required.

Although it's a small town, Chienge has a long history going back to pre-colonial times and spanning the colonial period when it served as a *boma* for imperial rulers.

During the slave trade, the area suffered a lot from the damage inflicted by Arab slave traders and their African counterparts.

The *boma* at Chienge was probably the first colonial post in what came to be known as North-Eastern Rhodesia. And it was one of the most remote outposts of the British Empire.

During British colonial rule, there was also a thriving trade in salt, besides fishing. The salt was deposited by streams flowing from the hills.

The Chienge *boma* was closed in 1933 and was superseded by Kawambwa and then Nchelenge *bomas*.

About 40 years later, Chienge was restored as a sub-administrative centre under Nchelenge District in the 1970s, and as a full administrative district in the 1990s.

The area was also severely affected by conflicts in neighbouring Congo through the years when tens of thousands of people sought refuge in the area. The United Nations High Commission for Refugees (UNHCR) established camps for them in Kawambwa District in Luapula Province and in Mporokoso District in the Northern Province.

And if there is a highly visible symbol of Chienge's predicament as a district, and there are many such symbols, it is the district's extremely poor infrastructure including roads. Such roads, good roads, simply don't exist. The district has a long way to go. As Austin Kaluba stated in his report, "Chienge District Still Lagging Behind," in the *Times of Zambia*:

"Picture yourself in an area without a phone, television facilities or easy means of transportation then you are close to describing Chienge district on the fringes of Luapula Province bordering the Democratic Republic of Congo.

Chienge district is a Rip-Van-Winkle town slumbering while other areas are advancing in communication.

Despite belonging to one of the most developed rural provinces in Zambia, Chienge has lagged behind in development.

The major hindrance has been the bad road which can only be likened to the notorious 1970's Hell Run (the Great North road).

While residents in Nchelenge enjoy a tarred road, their counterparts in Chienge have been cut off from civilisation by the bad road. From Kashikishi in Nchelenge to Lunchinda in Chienge, the road is very dusty and bumpy.

Apart from the bad road, Chienge suffers from lack of infrastructure and poor communication facilities in the district which despite having electricity has not been a favourite place for many Government workers.

The lack of reliable communication has also led to incessant attacks from fleeing DR Congo soldiers and rebels who pose security threat to the residents from time to time.

Senior Chief Puta of the Bwile people in Chienge district has lamented the lack of security in the district and called on the Government to establish a barrack in Lunchinda area on the border with DR.

Chief Puta said in an interview there was need to find a permanent solution instead of sending soldiers to the district only when there is a security problem.

He said the war in the neighbouring DR Congo was

likely to take long and there was need for a permanent barrack to keep ruthless soldiers and rebels at a distance.

'People in Chienge and Kaputa districts have never enjoyed peace like their counterparts in other parts of Zambia because of the imminent fear of attacks from Congolese soldiers.'

He said the establishment of a barrack in the area would also help to control the possession of arms which have found themselves in wrong hands.

'A number of locals now have arms which they use for poaching and committing criminal activities. They obtain these arms from fleeing soldiers from DRC,' the chief said.

Chienge police officer in-charge Gibson Chisala who was speaking at the council offices also called on the Government to beef up security in the district.

Mr Chisala said the police was experiencing numerous difficulties including under-staffing, lack of transport and decent accommodation.

Mr Chisala said the common cases the police were handling had to do with witchcraft and illegal possession of fire arms.

'The other problem is the large number of Congolese nationals some of them who are involved in criminal activities which the understaffed police station cannot handle,' he said.

Mr Chisala said refugees from DR Congo troop in weekly from Mpweto and after being screened at Chienge refugee transit camp, they are taken to refugee camps like Kala in Kaputa.

The Congolese in Chienge district and other parts of Luapula Province are called derogatory names like Abena Malungu or Ba Congolais.

Chienge council secretary Fred Banda said lack of good roads has been the major problem that has hampered several developmental projects in the district.

Mr Banda has called on the Government to tar the road from Kashikishi in Nchelenge to Lunchinda in Chienge to ease transportation of people and goods to the district.

Mr Banda said despite the tarring of the road being included in the 2003-2006 Yellow book transition plan, there has been no follow up to the plan.

He said the Government had even contracted JJ Lowe and Phoenix as major contractors to start the project but no money had been released for work to start.

'The road is in a bad state despite being used to transport fish and rice to the Copperbelt. The distance from Nchelenge to Chienge is very short but because of the bad road, the route seems long and many motorists fear using it,' he said.

Mr Banda has also appealed to the ministry of Local Government and Housing to give the council a truck that would help in operations of the cash-strapped local authority.

Mr Banda said much was needed to make Chienge live up to the district status that was bestowed on it in 1996, especially in communication.

'Up to now, there is no TV or telephone in Chienge. The bad road has somehow contributed to the place being neglected. Plans are however underway to introduce CASAT to enable residents to watch . We are really cut off from civilisation because of the bad road,' he said.

Chienge district council chief administrative officer Musonda Chipenya said the council had written a letter to CASAT who said K78 million was needed to complete the TV project.

'We were requested to pay K300,000 registration fee which our area member of Parliament Katele Kalumba paid. We have not been updated on the project up to now,' he said.

Mr Banda also appealed to the Government to repair the derelict grader that is parked at the council offices and a starter panel water pump for smooth operations of council services provision.

'The funding from central Government is erratic to

enable us to operate effectively. The fish levy that we collect is gobbled up in paying salaries, paying of pensions and offering services to the residents,' he said.

The council secretary said the council has also appealed to the Government to provide flood lights at Puta and Mununga markets but the local authority was advised that Government has stopped providing such services.

Mr Banda also complained of lack of accommodation for Government workers disclosing that many were living in grass-thatched houses in nearby Kangalo, Natente and Puta villages.

'There is also lack of office accommodation. Many departments crowd in one office which has led to many ministries not being represented in Chienge district,' he said.

The Puta Health Centre is inadequate to cater for Chienge residents in offering health services. The centre has no mattresses and blankets forcing patients to sleep on the floor.

'Patients have to take their own blankets to the centre. The centre has no ambulance and all complicated cases are referred to St Pauls Mission in Nchelenge a distance of 106 km,' said Advent Mulolo Chisanga, a resident.

Another Chienge resident Bernard Chisanga also lamented the lack of a secondary school in the district where pupils who qualify to secondary school are referred to Nchelenge.

When this author visited the area, there were by-elections to replace the late councillor Jordan Mumba. MMD fielded Moffat Chansa while UPND had Goodson Mambwe as its candidate.

Chienge has two senior chiefs Puta and Mununga with their subordinates Chieftainess Lambwe Chomba, Chipungu, Kalembwe, Mukunta, Nshimba, Munkombwe and Mutampuka.

Chienge stretches along Lake Mweru from Mwatishi river to Lunchinda river on the border with DR Congo in the Northern part of Zambia.

Chienge consists of the Bwile people who celebrate the Ubwilile harvest ceremony and the Shila people in Mununga who celebrate the Mabila ceremony, a spiritual ceremony to honour ancestral spirits.

The name of the incarcerated Katele Kalumba dominates political discussions in the area.

Residents talk fondly of the politician who helped in developing the area.

If the road from Kashikishi to Lunchinda is tarred, Chienge will like other districts in Luapula Province enjoy the fruits of being linked to other towns along the line of rail." – (Austin Kaluba, "Chienge District Still Lagging Behind," in *Times of Zambia*, Ndola, Zambia, April 2007).

Kawambwa is another district in Luapula Province. Its capital is also known as Kawambwa.

The town of Kawambwa is located on the edge of the northern Zambian plateau above the Luapula Valley at an altitude of 4265 feet. It was chosen as an administrative district of the same name by the British colonial authorities who preferred the cooler climate at higher altitudes. They didn't like the valley where it's hotter. Most of the people in the district live in the valley.

Kawambwa sits at the junction of gravel roads to Nchelenge, Mporokoso, Mushota and Mansa, and a tarred road to Mbereshi linking with the Zambia Way which is the main tarred highway of Luapula Province that runs through Kazembe – also known as Mwansabombwe – and Mansa.

Zambia's largest tea plantation is located about 17 miles from Kawambwa on the Mporokoso road.

A camp for refugees who fled from the war in the eastern part of the Democratic Republic of Congo was established by United Nations agencies at Kala 15 miles north of Kawambwa in 1998 to accommodate 40,000 of them.

Another district in Luapula Province is Mansa. Its capital is also the capital of Luapula Province.

The name Mansa comes from the local Chief Mansa and the small Mansa River which flows west into the Luapula River. During British colonial rule, the town was called Fort Rosebery. It was also the headquarters of the province during that period.

But the first Fort Rosebery was not located at the site where Mansa is today. It was built in the Luapula valley around 1900 near Mambilima.

After an outbreak of sleeping sickness in the valley some years later, the provincial capital was moved to the present site because the colonial rulers felt that having the capital at a higher altitude was better in terms of health for the town's residents.

Most of the people in the province live in the Luapula valley.

The economic growth of Luapula Province in the mid-1900s was fuelled by trade in fish, agricultural production, and provision of labour to the mines on the Copperbelt, the country's industrial hub. This also led to the development of Mansa as the main administrative and distribution centre for the region.

During the past two decades since the 1980s, the town of Mansa has grown considerably in terms of population. But there has been no parallel growth in terms of prosperity because of the decline of the copper industry, leading to loss of jobs in the mines. Many workers have been forced to return to the rural areas, and Luapula Province has been one of the hardest-hit.

Mansa does not have industries. Its most prominent manufacturing plant was a battery factory which was closed in 1994.

Unemployment is a major problem and many town residents have resorted to a form of subsistence farming known as *chitemene* for survival. But this has had a devastating impact on the environment. The surrounding woodlands have been destroyed, seriously affecting the ecological system.

Still, as the province's commercial centre, the town of Mansa plays an important role in the economy of the region. It has an infrastructure which includes important facilities and institutions such as banks, warehouses, many shops, a daily market, individual retailers, and a Shoprite supermarket.

The town is on a relatively featureless plateau between the Luapula River to the west and Lake Bangweulu to the east. Its location is a kind of a focal point because the town was built at the crossroads of the Copperbelt-Congo-Pedicle-Chembe-Kawambwa road running from south to north, and the Serenje-Samfya-Luapula valley road running from southeast to northwest.

Mansa is only 31 miles from the Democratic Republic of the Congo. And it's cut off from the Copperbelt by the Congo Pedicle. But it does not have direct trade links to Congo.

Also wars and other conflicts in Congo since the sixties – and just before Congo won independence – have had a direct impact on Mansa, impeding progress, especially economic development.

The Luapula River forms a boundary with Congo. It's served by a passanger ferry to the northwest at Kasenga and by a vehicle ferry to the south at Chembe. But this connection goes through Congolese territory via Zambia's notorious and frequently impassable Congo Pedicle road and only to the Copperbelt.

Roads on the Congolese side are even worse. Because of that, some Congolese trade passes on Zambian roads through Mansa. A typical example is copper from Dikulushi, a copper and silver mine in the Democratic Republic of Congo located 31 miles north of Kilwa in Katanga Province and 14 miles west of Lake Mweru.

Because of all these obstacles, trade between Mansa and Congo is restricted to local produce and smuggling across the river.

In 2010, a bridge was being built across the Luapula river at Chembe to bypass the ferry. But peace and stability in neighbouring Congo will be critical to the viability of this bridge. Conversely, conflict will disrupt transport. Also, paving the Pedicle Road will do a lot to improve Mansa's access to the Copperbelt and may also increase trade between Kasama and the Copperbelt.

Another district in Luapula Province is Milenge. The district capital is also called Milenge.

It's a very small town. It has a *boma* which comprises the district council and other offices. It's really a village. But it has a few thousand people.

Milenge is the most southerly district in Luapula Province. It was was carved out of Mansa District.

It's rural and does not have any infrastructure, not even one good road.

A single dirt road runs through the central part of the district from Chembe in the west to the provincial capital, Mansa.

The vast majority of the people in Milenge District live in the valley of the Lwela River. It's a shallow valley.

Next we look at Nchelenge. It's a district in the northern part of Luapula Province. Its capital is also called Nchelenge.

The town is located on the southeastern shore of Lake Mweru. It's connected to Kashikishi and the two towns are sometimes referred to as Nchelenge-Kashikishi because of this connection which makes them a "single" entity.

In addition to being the headquarters of Nchelenge District, the town of Nchelenge is also the administrative centre for the Zambian part of Lake Mweru. It's also the seat of the branches of national offices and institutions. Kashikishi, on the other end, is the market centre of the area.

Transport is rudimentary but there are ferries which sail from Nchelenge to Kilwa Island and Isokwe.

Kilwa Island is an island on Lake Mweru on the Zambian side. The island was known to Arab and Swahili traders of ivory, copper and slaves. They used Kilwa Island for some time as an operational base. And the name of the island probably came from an island in Tanzania also known as Kilwa; so did the name of a place also called Kilwa across the border in Katanga Province in the Democratic Republic of Congo (DRC).

The island in Tanzania is a small island located in the Indian Ocean in the southern part of the country. To distinguish it from other sites also known as Kilwa in that area, the island is called Kilwa Kisiwani, which is a Swahili or Kiswahili term meaning "Kilwa on the island." And because of the connection between Zambia and the coastal area of Tanzania established by the Arab and Swahili traders, that's probably why the island on Lake Mweru in Zambia is also named Kilwa Island.

Isokwe is another island on Lake Mweru in Luapula Province. It's about 3 miles from the town of Kashikishi which is located on the southeastern shore of the lake.

The long, narrow island is known for its fishing business and extends west into the Luapula swamps of the delta. And it's regularly visited by people from Nchelenge by ferry.

Kashikishi lies just north of the town of Nchelenge.

But while Nchelenge is the seat of the district government and branches of national offices, Kashikishi has earned a big reputation not only as as the market and fisheries centre but also as the economic hub of the district. Kashikishi also has the largest hospital in Nchelenge District which is run by the Roman Catholic Church.

The last district we are going to look at in Luapula Province is Samfya, and its capital which is also known as Samfya, located in the southeastern part of the province.

Like all districts, the capital of Samfya is the focal point in the district even though in many if not in most cases, district officials in the capitals of these districts don't do much or anything to help the people. The people are left on their own.

But also in many cases, these towns serve as centres of economic and political activities and other major events in the districts for no other reason than that they are the district headquarters. The town of Samfya in Samfya District in Luapula Province is no exception.

The town is located on the southwestern shore of Lake Bangweulu. The lake has crocodiles.

In addition to local government offices and branches of national offices being in Samfya, the small town also serves as a commercial and fishing centre. It's also a centre for transport by boat to islands and other areas of Lake Bangweulu. The hinterland areas include farms and some timber plantations.

The Kwanga Festival of the members of the Njumba tribe is held in Samfya in October every year just before the rainy season starts in November.

In addition to preserving rituals, customs and traditions, the festival is very important in strengthening ties among the members of the tribe who must see themselves as one people and as a cohesive entity.

From Luapula Province, we go to Lusaka Province.

Lusaka Province

Lusaka Province takes its name from the nation's capital Lusaka. In fact, it's the capital itself and its surroundings which constitute the core of this province in terms of population. The nation's capital is also the provincial capital of Lusaka Province.

Lusaka Province is divided into four districts: Chongwe, Kafue, Luangwa, and Lusaka.

Chongwe District is located 28 miles east of the nation's capital Lusaka. The capital of the district is also known as Chongwe.

The Great East Road leading to Zambia's Eastern Province and to Malawi and Mozambique goes through Chongwe District.

The district is sparsely populated. The highest concentrations of population are in the district capital and in farming areas in different parts of the district.

It's a rural district whose inhabitants depend on agriculture to earn a living, as is the case with most of the people in the rural areas across the country.

Also, as a rural district, the rate of poverty is higher than it is in urban areas. And the incidence of disease is higher than that of urban districts.

Diseases weaken the productive capacity of the people in the rural areas – as they do among urban dwellers – making it very difficult and sometimes even impossible for them to provide for themselves. And hunger due to crop failure compounds the problem.

Reliance on rain to grow crops is another risk the people must take in their struggle to survive. For a number of years, Chongwe District has had bad weather conditions, as have many other parts of Zambia, severely affecting productivity. Animal diseases have also added to the misfortune the people in the district have suffered through the years.

But in spite of all those problems, Chongwe District has a lot of potential in a number of areas to make it a prosperous area even if not in the near future.

The district has potential for tourism. It also has minerals and opportunities in other areas which have not been fully exploited.

Sand mining and quarrying are the major activities in the mining sector in the district. Chongwe District supplies very large quantities of building and river sand to Lusaka District.

But most of the sand mining is done by individual miners or by a few individuals working together on a small scale. And much of it is uncontrolled, threatening the environment and the district's already fragile infrastructure such as roads, including feeder roads.

There has also been some copper mining done in the district. Copper mining is done by companies but on a small scale. Sometimes companies are involved in medium-scale mining projects.

But it's agriculture which remains the backbone of the district's economy. Horticultural and livestock production are also important economic activities in the district.

More than 75 per cent of household incomes in Chongwe District are derived from crop production and related activities. People work on farms, they sell crops and other commodities, and they're involved in other activities related to agriculture – more than anything else – to earn a living.

The main crops grown in Chongwe District include maize, groundnuts, beans, peas, sweet potatoes, fruits , vegetables, cotton and sunflower.

Most of the farms are small-scale. But there is also commercial farming in the district.

After agriculture, the other major economic activity in Chongwe District is trading. This involves manufactured goods mainly from the nation's capital Lusaka – as well as other major urban centres but mostly from Lusaka – which are sold to the people in the districts in retail outlets usually owned and/or managed by individuals.

The retail outlets are mostly small shops. The outlets also include stalls and makeshift stands. In some parts of the district, for example, Chimusanya and Rufunsa, district authorities have market stalls rented out to traders.

In addition to trade in manufactured goods such as clothes, shoes, soap, toothpaste, medicine and other items sold to the people in the rural areas, the other common form of trading in the district involves farm products.

Most of the farm products sold are unprocessed. Some are semi-processed. Almost none are fully processed because of lack of technology and mass-production techniques commonly used in industrialised countries.

Chongwe District is a major source of agricultural commodities bought by the urban residents of the city of Lusaka which is less than 30 miles away from this rural district.

The district supplies the markets in Lusaka with a wide variety of agricultural products, mostly foods such as beans, peas, maize, cabbages, tomatoes, onions, pepper, fruits and other products.

Most of these are grown by small- and medium-scale farmers and are sold directly on farms or at farm gates or at markets in different parts of the district.

For the markets in the nation's capital Lusaka, it's usually large-scale farmers who supply the products for consumption by the city's residents. The main products they supply are livestock products, especially meat and milk, as well as eggs and poultry. Large-scale farmers in Chongwe District also provide horticultural products for the international market.

In terms of industrial production, Chongwe District lags far behind in that area. Formal industrial activity in the district is very low, mostly involving semi-processing of farm products.

But the informal sector is relatively strong across the district. It mainly involves processing farm products, for example, milling maize. There are also a number of carpentry shops in different parts of the district making and repairing furniture.

The pattern of these economic activities is virtually duplicated in other rural parts of Zambia, with Chongwe District being only a microcosm.

It's common to see women in Chongwe District – and in other parts of the country – by road sides selling a wide variety of foods including eggs, fruits, maize, groundnuts, beans and different kinds of vegetables and other agricultural products.

It's also women who sell food products and other commodities at different markets. But it's usually men who handle trade at the farm gates and in shops.

Chongwe District also has tourist attractions, some of them unique to the district. They include the Chinyunyu hot spring in Chinyunyu; ancient paintings in the caves in the Lukoshi area and surrounding hills like the Leopard Hills; game viewing in animal sanctuaries in Shikabeta; lodging and camping facilities at Chaminuka; and cultural ceremonies, especially Chakwela Makumbi, Nkomba Lyanga, and Chibwela Kumunshi.

Chakwela Makumbi is a celebration of the members of the Soli ethnic group.

It's an occasion when they ask their ancestors to intercede with the Almighty, on their behalf, so that they can be blessed with plenty of rain for their crops. As Elias Mbao, a correspondent of the Kenyan newspaper, *Daily Nation*, stated in his report from Chongwe, Zambia, "President at Ritual to Plead for Rains":

"Zambian leader Rupiah Banda on Saturday joined local chiefs in a traditional ritual to ask ancestral spirits and God for rains.

Officiating at Chakwela Makumbi traditional ceremony, which means pulling clouds together to form rains, of the Soli people in Chongwe District, about 45km east of Lusaka, President Banda implored Zambians to produce a bumper harvest through hard work, discipline and prayers to God.

'Your royal highness, not only have you prayed for us to have rains so that we can have a lot of food, but you are telling us in the same spirit that we can only have food if we work hard. I remember you telling me, as we were planting there, that this ceremony marks the end of pleasure of wearing suits as we are dressed today, that now we must get ready to go to work,' said President Banda.

The ceremony was attended by about 17 chiefs from

various parts of Zambia....

Other than being a ritual to ask for rains, President Banda said the Chakwela Makumbi traditional ceremony unifies Zambians.

'It is such a wonderful treat to see Zambians from all walks of life, tribes and cultures coming together to celebrate the Chakwela Makumbi ceremony,' said President Banda.

Earlier, President Banda and the head of the Soli people, Senior Chieftainess Nkomeshya Mukamambo II, lit a fire to clear a crop field and planted maize and other food crops within her palace after the chieftainess' ritual prayer to the ancestors.

The essence of this traditional ceremony is to ask our ancestral spirits to give my people rains and other favourable weather conditions to enable them grow and harvest enough food,' said Nkomeshya Mukamambo II.

'Today, I stand here to pray to God to open up the windows of heaven so that the sky can shower the earth with the right amount of rains so that people can grow more food for themselves to eat. This is the uniqueness of my ceremony.'

President Banda was shown several local farming tools the Soli people have used to produce their food since time im memorial." – (Elias Mbao, "President at Ritual to Plead for Rains," *Daily Nation*, Nairobi, Kenya, 1 November 2009).

According to another report about this traditional ceremony:

"Traditional ceremonies are a unifying factor in Zambia, President Rupiah Banda has said. And senior chieftainess Nkomeshya Mukamambo II has urged the government to increase the number of fertiliser given to small scale farmers and upgrade Chalimbana Teacher in-service training College into a university.

Speaking at the Chakwela Makumbi traditional ceremony of the Soli people in Chongwe on Saturday, President Banda said traditional ceremonies bring people from all walks of life together.

'We should be proud of this heritage because culture is the means by which a people express itself through language, traditional wisdom, religion, art, music, tools, greetings, symbols, festivals, ethics, values and collective identity. Without culture, a community loses self-awareness and guidance, and grows weak and vulnerable,' President Banda said. 'Our rich cultural heritage should also be used to promote national unity.

The challenge for the Soli people and indeed for all Zambians is to preserve cultural events like this one as they serve as important fora through which the community can learn and assimilate useful customs, values and attitudes.'

He said the government was committed to supporting traditional ceremonies because there could be no meaningful development without culture.

'The challenge for us is to harness the potential of these cultural activities to create jobs for our people especially in rural areas,' he said....

'As a custodian of our cultural heritage, I implore you (Chieftainess Nkomeshya) to bring to the attention of your subjects issues pertaining to contemporary agricultural methods, girl child education, early marriages, HIV and AIDS, risky traditional practices such as sexual cleansing, spouse inheritance and spouse battering,' President Banda said.

President Banda commended paramount chief Chitimukulu of the Bemba people for traveling all the way to Chongwe despite his poor health, and other traditional rulers from various parts of Zambia.

Chakwela Makumbi, literary meaning gathering clouds to bring rains, is a ceremony where chieftainess Nkomeshya asks ancestral spirits to provide rains to her people." – ("Maravi: Traditional Ceremonies Are A Unifying Factor.").

Chakwela Makumbi is celebrated by members of the Soli tribe in Chongwe in November.

Another traditional ceremony in Chongwe District is Nkomba Lyanga which we will look at briefly since we have already taken a look at Chakwela Makumbi in some detail as a microcosm of the traditional ceremonies and festivals in Zambia. There are more than 30 such ceremonies in different parts of the country.

Nkomba Lyanga is also celebrated by the members of the Soli tribe. It's held at the palace of the royal highness in Chongwe in July. It marks the beginning of the new planting season in October/November. The people also have a ceremony to thank the ancestors for the good harvest.

Chibwela Kumunshi is another traditional ceremony performed by the same people, the Soli; at the same place, the royal palace, and for the same purpose but at a different time. It's also attended by leading traditional rulers and government officials including the president of Zambia:

"President Rupiah Banda has called for enhanced public-private partnership in the promotion and preservation of traditional ceremonies because of their non-partisan nature.

President Banda said government will continue to encourage the holding of traditional ceremonies for the benefits of the children, youths and tourists to assimilate traditional values.

Mr Banda said in a speech read for him by Lusaka Province Minister, Charles Shawa during the 2009 Chibwela Kumunshi traditional ceremony of the Soli people of Chief Bundabunda of Chongwe district yesterday (30 August 2009)....

Senior Chieftainess Nkomeshya Mukamambo II, Chieftainess Shikabeta and representatives for Senior Chief Mburuma and Mpamshya and Chongwe Member of Parliament Sylvia Masebo, attended the ceremony.

The Chibwela Kumunshi traditional ceremony of the Soli people of Chief Bundabunda is held to cerebrate and thank ancestral spirits for a good harvest in the last farming season." – ("Rupiah Calls For Enhanced Public-Private Partnership," QFM Radio, Lusaka, Zambia, Monday, 31 August 2009).

After Chongwe District, we look at another one of the four districts which collectively constitute Lusaka Province. We look at Kafue District next.

Kafue is one of the most well-known districts in Zambia. The district capital or headquarters is also named Kafue and is one of the most well-known towns in Zambia although it's not one of the largest.

The town of Kafue is located on the northern bank of Kafue River. It's named after the river.

The town is the southern gateway to the central Zambian plateau on which Lusaka and the mining towns of Kabwe and the Copperbelt are located.

Agriculture and fishing are the main economic activities around the town of Kafue. And there is a commercial farming area that stretches for about 22 miles northwest of the town along the edge of the Kafue flats.

The town of Kafue also has a larger proportion of manufacturing industries than most of other towns outside the Copperbelt. The industries include: textiles; Nitrogen Chemicals of Zambia making fertilisers for crops and other agricultural products; and a shoe leather company called Bata Tannery. Kafue also has an industrial estate with housing and services called Kafue Estates.

Other industries in or near the town include Kafue Fisheries Ltd. Whose activities include pig farming besides fishing; a game farm with a tourist lodge; and

Kafue Quarry which produces construction aggregate for road building and general construction.

The town also has the Kafue Gorge Dam, about 18-and-a-half miles downstream, generating electricity. The dam also helps the city to store water after the end of the rainy season by forming a water reservouir.

Luangwa is another district in Lusaka Province. Its capital is also named Luangwa. The original settlement was founded by the Portuguese as we learnt earlier when we looked at the town of Luangwa.

Like all the other districts in the country, the district headquarters is the district's nerve centre by the mere fact that it's the capital.

Many decisions affecting the district come from the centre, which is the district centre or capital. But these decisions are, normally, not made at the district level. They're simply handed down to the grassroots level because, like all the other African countries, Zambia is a highly centralised state. Most decisions going all the way down to the grassroots level are made at the highest levels; which means at the national level and next at the regional level.

But, in spite of all that, district capitals play an important role in the lives of the people if for no other reason than that they are the centres of all important activities in the districts.

Lusaka is the last district on the list of the districts which collectively constitute Lusaka Province.

The district is made up of Lusaka, the nation's capital, and its surrounding areas. The capital virtually constitutes the district. It's also this metropolitan area which is the core of Lusaka Province itself.

The nation's capital is also the capital of Lusaka District. And we are going to look at it in the next part of the book which focuses on the nation's largest urban centres.

Although Lusaka Province is largely urban because of

of the nation's capital Lusaka being the core of the province and the area with the largest population, it also has havens for wild animals.

Next we're going to look at the Northern Province.

Northern Province

The Northern Province covers approximately one fifth of Zambia in land area. The provincial capital is Kasama.

Kasama grew considerably in the 1970s and 1980s after the Tanzania-Zambia Railway (TAZARA) was built. It passes through Kasama..

The town's growth was also facilitated by the improvement of the Great North Road which was tarred from Mpika through Kasama to Mbala.

Kasama is located at the centre of a road network which extends to Luapula Province in the west, Mporokoso in the northwest, Isoka in the east, and Kayambi in the northeast, making it a commercial hub of a large region, providing services in banking, marketing and in other areas. It also has an airport.

The town is in the heartland of Bemba territory, inhabited by members of the Bemba ethnic group. Their Paramount Chief Chitimukulu has his headquarters about 31 miles from Kasama.

The British established a *boma* at Kasama during colonial rule. The town's central location and its proximity to Chitimukulu's royal residence led to the town eventually becoming the largest and most important urban centre in the northeastern region of what became the colony of Northern Rhodesia.

There is also Stone Age rock art near the town. The Chishimba Falls are also near Kasama.

The Northern Province is composed of 12 districts. They are Kasama whose district headquarters is also the provincial capital; Chilubi, Isoka, Chinsali, Kaputa,

Luwingu, Mbala, Mporokoso, Mpika, Mpulungu, Mungwi and Nakonde.

The province is widely considered to be the homeland of the Bemba, one of the largest tribes in Zambia.

Prominent features of Northern Province include part of Lake Tanganyika which is shared with Tanzania, the Democratic Republic of Congo and Burundi; Lake Bangweulu and its wetlands, Lake Mweru-wa-Ntipa, and a number of waterfalls including Lumangwe Falls, Kabwelume Falls, Chishimba and Kalambo Falls.

The province has a lot of potential for tourism which has fuelled economic growth in other parts of Zambia. But poor infrastructure and vast distances between major points of interest in the province make visiting this part of the country difficult.

The Northern Province is the largest of Zambia's 9 provinces. It shares borders not only with three other provinces – Central, Eastern, and Luapula – but also with three countries: the Democratic Republic of Congo (DRC) in the north, Tanzania in the northeast, and Malawi in the east.

The Northern Province is also the source of the Congo River, the second-longest on the continent after the Nile River.

The Northern Province also has the highest population growth rate among all the nine provinces. And the provincial capital Kasama has the highest percentage of population among all the 12 districts in the province.

The rapid annual population growth in the Northern Province is attributed to various factors. For instance, the high growth rate in Nakonde is attributed to the free cross-border trade between Zambia and Tanzania which has led to an influx of a large number of people who have settled in the district.

The high economic potential of the Chambeshi River valley, especially in agriculture, explains the rapid growth rate in Mungwi, while part of the population growth for

Mporokoso is attributed to the influx of refugees from the Democratic Republic of Congo.

The Northern Province has various tribal or ethnic groups. They speak different languages but the language mostly spoken across the province is Bemba, or *IsiBemba*, which in my natitve Nyakyusa language is known as *IkiBemba*.

It's the native language of the largest ethnic group in the province, the Bemba, who live mostly in Chinsali, Kasama, Mungwi and parts of Mporokoso and Luwingu districts.

Other prominent languages spoken in the Northern Province include Bisa which is spoken by the members of the Bisa tribe of Mpika and Chilubi; *IsiNamwanga* spoken by the Namwanga people of Nakonde and Isoka districts; *ChiTumbuka* spoken by the Tumbuka of Isoka; and *IsiMambwe* spoken by the members of the Mambwe tribe of Mbala District.

But in spite its size and the diversity of languages as well as dialects, the Northern Province is home to a diverse group of people who generally share a common culture, although there are significant tribal differences even in this cultural commonwealth.

Each of the tribes in the province has its own traditional leadership headed by either a paramount chief or a senior chief assisted by junior chiefs and village headmen.

The most prominent chief in the province is Chitimukulu, the Paramount Chief of the Bemba.

The Northern Province is a cultural stronghold, rich in customs and traditions, cultural institutions and traditional centres of power. But it has no industries. Its economy is based almost entirely on agriculture.

The most important crops are maize, millet, sorghum, groundnuts, beans, and rice. Most of the food produced is consumed within the province. But a small percentage is sold. Agricultural commodities which are sold are bought by traders who sell the products at market stands and trading centres along the railway.

Most of the farming is subsistence. There are very few farmers who grow crops on a commercial basis in the Northern Province.

Subsistence farming is usually very simple, using traditional methods including slash-and-burn techniques prevalent in many parts of the continent. Other methods include shifting cultivation, known as *chitemene*, and sometimes combined with modern techniques here and there. But productivity is low and many people don't even produce enough for themselves.

Fishing is another important economic activity in the area, mainly on Lake Tanganyika. There are individual fishermen. There are also companies which do commercial fishing on Lake Tanganyika. The companies are based in Mpumulungu, a port on Lake Tanganyika.

Most of the fish caught are sold in the nation's capital Lusaka and in the towns and cities on the Copperbelt. They're transported in refrigerated trucks.

Small-scale fishermen sell their small catches to local traders and others who resell the fish in the nearby towns of Mbala and Kasama.

Mpumulungu, where fishing companies are based, is located 129 miles from the regional capital Kasama. It's Zambia's only port. And its harbour is generally used to export bulky goods – such as sugar and cement – to Burundi, Rwanda and the Democratic Republic of Congo. In turn, Zambia also imports small, dried fish – *kapenta* – and other merchandise from these countries and from Tanzania through the same port.

Lake Tanganyika has one of the most diverse fish populations in the world. There are also many crocodiles and hippos in the lake.

Although the Northern Province has very poor communication infrastructure, the situation changed somewhat when telecommunication facilities which were obsolete were improved in 2005 with the introduction of cellular phone services in all 12 districts in the province.

Before then, the situation was so bad that it was easier to make a telephone call outside the province than to any other district within the province. But cellular phone services are expensive.

The Northern Province has only about 560 miles of tarmac roads. Most of them need to be repaired. The rest are gravel roads. They're also very bad and almost impassable.

The province has a number of game parks and other animal sanctuaries but some of them have been seriously affected by the wars in neighbouring Congo through the years, mainly because of the influx of refugees fleeing the conflicts. They have sought refuge in some of the wildlife areas for many years.

One of the parks, the Mweru Wantipa National Park, has also witnessed an influx of people engaged in fishing. There has been very little protection for the park, especially in the western part where there has been no management for decades. The park is fair ground for everybody and could suffer severely from environmental and ecological destruction if the situation is not improved soon.

Although the province is very underdeveloped, and remote, it has one important connection to the outside world. And that is the international aquarium trade because of the wide variety of fish obtained from Lake Tanganyika, a part of which is in the province.

The first district we're going to look at in the Northern Province is Chilubi and its capital.

Chilubi District covers the northeastern part of Bangweulu Lake and Bangweulu Swamps containing several islands including Chilubi Island and some of the mainland northeast of the lake.

Like Samfya District, most of the district is lake or swamp, and the rest rural and less developed than Samfya, lacking roads and infrastructure.

Channels have been cut through the swamps in many places to help with navigation by boat.

Since they share the lake and swamps, Chilubi District does, geographically, have more in common with Samfya District in Luapula Province than it does with the rest of Northern Province in which it is located.

Islands in Chilubi District which are at the edges of the swamps form a very important link to the mainland when they become dry during the dry season.

Another district in the Northern Province is Chinsali. The district headquarters is also Chinsali.

It has the unique distinction of being the home of the founding fathers of Zambia: President Kenneth Kaunda and Vice President Simon Kapwepwe who was also his childhood friend.

Kenneth Kaunda was born at Lubwa Mission in the small town of Chinsali on 28 April 1924. And Simon Kapwepwe was also born in the district of Chinsali on 12 April 1922. He attended primary school in the town of Chinsali where he met Kenneth Kaunda but also had ties to Luwingu District.

The country estate of Shiwa Ngandu is also located in Chinsali District. The mansion built on the estate is an architectural achievement of magnificent splendour in the midst of nowhere. The entire estate is a transplant of Western civilisation in a traditional African society of the Bemba people.

The name Shiwa Ngandu, also spelled Shiwa Ng'andu, comes from a small lake nearby, Lake Ishiba Ng'andu, which in the Bemba language means "lake of the royal crocodile." The mansion itself is also known as "Shiwa House."

Construction of the mansion began in 1920 when what is now Zambia was the British colony of Northern Rhodesia. The building was completed in the late 1950s. When the work was completed, facilities on the estate included nursery gardens, and tennis courts, among other things.

The project was conceived and directed by Stewart Gore-Brown who became one of the most influential British settlers in Northern Rhodesia. He was also a close friend of Kenneth Kaunda who later became the first president of Zambia.

His political career began in 1935 when he was elected a member of Northern Rhodesia's Legislative Council. And from 1938 to 1951, he represented African interests in the legislative council as a nominated member.

He died from pneumonia at Kasama Hospital in Kasama, Northern Province, on 4 August 1967. He was buried at Shiwa Ng'andu two days later. It was a state funeral. President Kaunda gave the eulogy.

The state he established is one of the most outstanding monuments in Zambia; and a witness to history, colonial and post-colonial. It has also permanently placed the Northern Province in the spotlight despite the province's reputation as one of the most "backward" regions in the entire country.

From Chinsali, we go to Isoka District.

Isoka is another district in the Northern province. Its capital is also known as Isoka.

Members of the Namwanga, Mambwe, Tumbuka and Nyika ethnic groups are some of the people who live in Isoka District. They're also some of the major tribes in Zambia.

Next is Kaputa District. Its capital is also called Kaputa.

The district is located at the northern end of the Northern Province bordering the Democratic Republic of Congo. And because of its proximity to Congo, it has suffered from the conflicts next-door which have spilled into the district. According to a report from Kaputa by Zambian journalist Edward Mulenga, "Mai Mai Burn Kaputa Villages," in the *Times of Zambia*, 7 July 2003:

"Hundreds of people have fled into the bush after suspected Mai Mai militiamen from the Democratic Republic of Congo (DRC) burnt down three villages along the Zambian border and grabbed property from residents in Kaputa district at the weekend (5 – 6 July 2003).

District administrator Emmanuel Chileshe said in an interview yesterday from Kaputa that the security situation was deteriorating everyday, despite recent military reinforcements to the area."

The people in the district also share ethnic, cultural, historical and social ties with their counterparts across the border in Congo.

We now go to Kasama District. It surrounds the provincial capital of Kasama which also serves as the district headquarters.

Luwingu is another district in the Northern Province. It's well-endowed in terms of agricultural potential and other resources but lags far behind because of very poor infrastructure – which doesn't even exist in most parts of the district.

One very important part of this infrastructural network is roads. They're very poor and would serve the district very well if they were improved and new ones built to create a reliable road network. According to a report, "Luwingu Road Construction Gains Ground," in the *Times of Zambia*:

"Lubingu, whose name with the passage of time has changed to Luwingu, has for a while been dogged by a poor road network whose effect has left this rich district to slumber in terms of agriculture.

Luwingu is situated about 160 kilometers west of Kasama, the provincial capital of Northern Province and shares boundaries with seven other districts.

In the north are Kasama and Mporokoso, Chilubi in the

south, Samfya in the south-west, Mansa and Mwense in the west and Kawambwa in the north-west.

The district is approximately 9,000 square kilometers and has a population of about 83,369 . Luwingu has been increasing its agriculture portfolio but for the poor road network which has hampered the delivery of farming products.

One has to go to Luwingu to have a first hand experience of what potential the district has and how that could contribute to national development if given the necessary support.

This potential can only be tapped through the establishment of a good road network to link the farmers to the Copperbelt and Kasama. Little wonder then that some places have been nicknamed Soweto or Kamwala because of heightened farming activities and the availability of quality farming products.

And having noted the need for good communication, the Kasama-Luwingu road which is currently being worked on by Sable Construction Company once completed will contribute to the change of the face of the district but that needs some supporting infrastructure in terms of feeder roads, which will enable easy access to areas where most of the farming was done which has taken abnormally long to be completed.

Luwingu acting district commissioner, Hassan Siambelele, observed that people in the district were prepared to turn the area into a food basket but with the necessary help from the Government.

Mr Siambelele said in an interview that, although people were using human labour in their fields, the district was every year recording an increase both in maize and beans yields, a situation reflected by the increased number of traders from across the country who go to buy farm products from the area.

Mr Siambelele also said that this year alone the Government had already distributed over 4,400 Urea and the same quantity of Basal dressing fertiliser bags compared to last year when the district received only half of the quantity.

The acting district commissioner added that the Food Reserve Agency (FRA) had by Press time already bought 30,922 x 50Kg bags and some more 60,000 were being collected from the areas which are far away from Luwingu boma.

'I am happy that FRA is on the ground buying the maize which is the main crop in the area and my appeal is that if the district can find buyers who can buy beans as well from farmers because at the moment some people are coming to the area to buy the commodity at very low price.

We are also appealing to the Government to build a farmers training center which will make most of our farmers go into cash crop farming. This is because potential farmers seem to have diverted their interest to fishing. That has unfortunately resulted into an increased number of people being attacked by crocodiles,' Mr Siambelele said.

He said money for the construction of a farmers training center had already been sourced and that the ministry of Lands had already allocated a place where to build the institution and what was remaining was a go ahead from the relevant authorities.

Luwingu residents are happy with the prospects of the district because animals like cows would be introduced in the area, which to a large extent would reduce the use of human labour for farming and increase yields in the district.

Mr Siambelele also commended the Government for funding the Kasama-Luwingu road project which, when completed would turn round the farming record of the district.

He said he was happy that the contractor of the road, Sable Transport and Construction has been on site for more than three years and in addition had done a lot of community work.

'At times it pays to have a local construction company doing the work because had it been for a foreign company, they would have abandoned the work if not paid on time.

But the contractor decided not to leave the job because the owners who are Zambians know and understand the problems afflicting our country and he has waited and now work is going on well,' he said.

Adding his sentiments to the state of Luwingu district, Chief Chipalo of the Bemba people in the district said construction of the roads in the area should not be politicised because doing so would disadvantage the would-be beneficiaries.

He said so far the road construction was gong on very well and people were happy with it and he too was happy that the contractor has listened to his advice of employing locals.

'When this contractor came I told him that since you are coming to my area I don't want to see imported labour since I have men here who can do the job who live right in this district. He is good because he did exactly as I requested him to.

And my people are now working for the company. I am also happy that the company has come to stay with us because it even asked for land here. I in return gave it a farming land on condition that local people should be employed,' the chief said.

The traditional ruler commended the Government for its agriculture policies and said that as a district, Luwingu had taken up that good move to improve its record in agriculture.

He said the Government under the Fertiliser Support Programme (FSP) had really motivated people to go into farming.

The contractor of the Kasama-Luwingu road said it was prepared to continue turning the gears of construction machinery should resources permit.

Sable Transport and Construction Limited managing director, Iqbal Alloo, said his company was committed to complete the road if the funds were available.

He explained that the commitment of the company to live up to its contractual obligations was evidenced by the fact that it has been on site for several years and did its work contractually.

'The completion of that road depends on the availability of funds because as for us we have always been ready for the job. That is why we are still on site since we signed the contract.

We are hoping that since the country has now reached the HIPC completion point, all will be okay and the road will be completed soon,' Mr Alloo said.

On its part, the Government said Kasama-Luwingu road was on its priority list and occupied the top slot because of its expected impact on the economy of Luwingu district.

Works and Supply Permanent Secretary, Biswayo Nkunika, said that the Government was committed to make sure that some inter-district roads were also well worked on.

He said Kasama-Luwingu road was one of the roads that the Government wants to be completed very soon.

'As the Government, we are geared to see one of the important road in the country that is Kasama-Luwingu road which will make it easy for transportation of farm products in Northern province.

We are also happy that the contractor is on site doing the work and very soon the roads will be complete,' Mr Nkunika said.

Luwingu as Lubingu is popularly known is definitely a yawning giant waiting for a massive prod to get it out of its slumber.

And once that potential is harnessed and fully realised the district will be a force to reckon with not only in the northern part of the country but a gem that would help to propel Zambia towards becoming the regional food basket." – (Raphael Simanego, "Luwingu Road Construction Gains Ground," in the *Times of Zambia*, Ndola, Zambia).

Another district in the Northern Province is Mbala. Its capital is also named Mbala and stands out among the country's urban centres for one reason.

It's Zambia's most northerly large town and occupies a strategic location close to the border with Tanzania, controlling the southern approaches to Lake Tanganyika about 25 miles by road to the northeast where the port of Mpulungu is located.

Once known as Abercorn during British colonial rule, Mbala was a key outpost in colonial administration of this part of south-central Africa.

The town is a part of the western Great Rift Valley and is prone to earthquakes.

Also the second highest waterfall in Africa, Kalambo Falls, is only about 25 miles northwest of Mbala.

Mbala is on the old Great North Road about 103 miles north of Kasama, the regional capital, and at one time was the end of that road. The road is paved but still in poor condition.

Mbala is located about 16 miles from the border with Tanzania.

There are also a number of archaeological sites in Mbala and around the town showing human activity in the area spanning thousands of years.

During World War I, Mbala was the centre of intense military activity involving German and British forces. The Germans had established themselves there during the war but the British failed to dislodge them.

After Germany surrendered, the commander of the German forces in East Africa, von Lettow-Vorbeck, formally surrendered at Mbala on 25 November 1918. He moved there from Tanganyika – German East Africa – to continue fighting.

There is a memorial about a mile southwest of the centre of town which marks the area where the German commander surrendered to the British, marking the end of the bloodiest war in modern world history.

When the Germans surrendered, they were ordered by the British to throw their guns and ammunition into Lake Chila which is located in the town of Mbala.

After Zambia won independence in 1964, the name of the town was changed from Abercorn to Mbala.

Mbala has a lot of potential. But this potenntial has not been fully exploited because of logistical problems and infrastructural limitations.

The area of Mbala is very fertile. It also has plenty of water. But it's too far from urban markets to sell its abundant agricultural products.

Similarly, while it has a lot of tourist potential, it's far from the main tourist routes. The main highway is in poor condition. And lack of regular air services discourage visitors.

Also, conflicts and other forms of strife on the shores of Lake Tanganyika in neighbouring Congo have interfered with trade and tourism on the lake, making it almost impossible for Mbala and Mpulungu to take advantage of their strategic location and potential as commercial centres.

Some of the attractions in the town of Mbala include the Moto-Moto Museum which is a museum of the Bemba culture (*moto* means fire in Kiswahili or Swahili which I also speak); the Mutomolo harvest thanksgiving ceremony at Lake Chila; and Uringa Pans.

Another district in the Northern Province is Mpika. It's capital is also named Mpika.

The town is located at the junction of the Great North Road to Kasama and Mbala and the Tanzam highway to Dar es Salaam, Tanzania. It also has station on the

TAZARA Railway.

The town of Mpika is near Lwitikila Falls. And the Nachikufu cave which contains rock art from the Neolithic age and thereafter is located south of Mpika.

Mporokoso is another district in the Northern Province. The district headquarters is also called Mporokoso. The name is also spelled and pronounced as "Mpolokoso" and "Mumpolokoso."

The town is named after Chief Mpolokoso, a senior chief of the Bemba people whose palace is located in the town.

Many refugees from the war in neighbouring Congo have sought refuge in the area through the years. The refugee camp administered by the United Nations High Commission for Refugees (UNHCR) is located at Mwange about 20 miles west of the town of Mporokoso.

Mpulungu District is another one of the 12 districts in the Northern Province. The district headquarters, also called Mpulungu, is located at the southern tip of Lake Tanganyika.

Mpumulungu is Zambia's only port. Therefore the country is not completely landlocked, although it mostly is.

From Mpulungu, boats sail to Congo, Tanzania and Burundi. The MV Liemba ferry – owned by Tanzania – sails from Mpulungu to Kasanga and Kigoma in western Tanzania with connections from there to Burundi's capital Bujumbura.

Mpulungu is also a fishing port and lies at the end of the old Great North Road.

Mungwi is another district in the Northern Province. It's located in the heart of the province and has a rich history of cultural institutions of the Bemba people.

It's a poor district but has a lot of potential. As Zambian journalist Anthony Mulowa stated in his article, "District Status Inspires Mungwi," in the country's leading newspaper the *Times of Zambia*:

"Down in the heart of Northern Province is a tiny district called Mungwi which was awarded district status in 1997.

Before that, Mungwi created as a farming block in the olden days, was administered by Kasama Municipal Council. Long before it achieved the status of being a district in the sixties and seventies, Mungwi was popularly known for having one of the best technical high schools in the country, Mungwi Secondary school.

Mungwi shares boundaries with Mbala in the North, Isoka and Nakonde in the Northeast, Chinsala in the southeast and Kasama in the west and has a population of 134,647.

Besides the education aspect, this new district has also a rich cultural background of the Bemba speaking people as it is a home of three traditional chiefs.

Mungwi district is the home of the Paramount Chief Chitimukulu, Chief Makasa and Chimbola.

That said about Mungwi, the upcoming district's main economic activities comprise farming, trading and fishing.

A recent tour of the district revealed that the district was determined to have the standards of the district uplifted despite various hardships it faced.

Agriculture

Mungwi has three types of farming systems: commercial, emergent and subsistence.

Acting District Commissioner Fanwell Bwembya said there were approximately 17,057 farmers out of which five were commercial, cultivating a total of 315 hectares, Emergent farmers are cultivating 910 hectares, while the small scale farmers pegged at 16,922 were utilising 12,458 hectares.

He named the major commercial farmers as African Plantation Company in Ngoli which produces coffee,

Kalungwishi sugar plantation in Nseluka, Kansolo farmers in Malolo and Nakatende farms.

Crop production and food security in the district is generally below the optimal level due to a number of factors such as poor soil fertility, inability by farmers to access fertilisers, and pest attacks especially for cassava and beans.

On average, Mr Bwembya said an emergent farmer in the district produced about 4,800 kg of maize against the standard 5,000 kg while small scale farmers produced about 3,000 kg of maize against an optimum of 4,320 kg.

Mungwi has four agricultural blocks namely Mungwi central, Chambeshi, Chamfumu and Kayambi which were divided in 22 agricultural camps.

Mr. Bwembya said there were three main organisations which were rendering agricultural support.

He said Cinci Wababili Rural Development Project owned by the Catholic brothers of Sacred Heart catered for 12,000 households in 104 villages.

The Programme Against Malnutrition (PAM) also distributed inputs to vulnerable farmers who were viable.

The Agriculture Support Programmes funded by the Swedish government was also one of the programmes meant to support agriculture in the district and had been in existence since 2003.

On livestock production, Mr Bwembya said the farmers in the district kept cattle, goats, sheep, chicken and pigs but the production levels were low due to disease outbreaks and poor management.

Land and use

Most of the land in the district is under the traditional leaders.

Mr Bwembya said the council only controlled a fraction of the land which is restricted to the area around the townships.

The power to issue of land for agricultural purposes is under the custodian of the traditional leaders.

Mungwi which was created as a farming block is surrounded by small land holdings which most of them are undeveloped.

Mr Bwembya said the district administration with the ministry of agriculture has embarked on accessing the developed and undeveloped land with the view of reposing and reallocating as per land act.

He said it was the Government policy to create land through the programme known as the Triangle of Hope (TOH) in an attempt to attract investors.

The land creation would be done in consultation with the ministry of Lands, Local Authority, Ministry of Agriculture and Traditional leaders.

'Once completed, this will solve the issue of lack of land for investments and possibly attract foreign investors in our district. Otherwise there is plenty of land which is not developed,' he said.

Tourism

Mungwi has great tourism potential although not exploited to the fullest.

The rich traditional ceremony of the Bemba people (Ukusefya Pa ngwena) remains one of the biggest events which attracts scores of tourists every year.

The district commissioner attributed to poor performance of the industry due to poor road and communication network.

He said other tourist attractions included heritage sites of rock paintings.

He said Kayambi mission was also another site where there are slave trade cells and the Catholic Church which has clocked more than 100 years.

'We need to sensitise and empower the local investors to enable them participate in tourism ventures,' he said.

Road Infrastructure

The district, through the Road Development Agency (RDA), is rehabilitating four feeder roads which are situated in Agricultural production areas.

The Mukosa road via Chilombwa, Mwamba, Mulilo a 45-km stretch was being worked on.

Pafwana feeder road a stretch of 10 km, Chewe feeder road which runs off D18 and Kafyama road off U7 will be rehabilitated under the RDA.

The works will however, be completed before the on set of the rainy season.

On trunk roads, Mr Bwembya said the D18 which is the Kasama-Isoka road (via Mbsesuma pontoon) were awaiting tender procedures to be completed while D3-Nseluka (via Kayambi to Nakonde) which is in a deplorable state would be worked on once the Government released funds.

He said this was an important road as it passed through high agricultural production areas and the Government was keen to ensure that the road was rehabilitated and a sum of K1 billion had been set aside.

Education

Famous for its technical school, it is the district's aim through the ministry of education to achieve an effective and efficient delivery of education services through equitable provision of quality free education and increase access to higher formal education.

The district commissioner said learning institutions in the district had increased from 103 last year to 118 which included two high schools and 15 community schools.

Mr Bwembya said the enrolment of boys and girls stood at 36,702 saying the rate at which girls dropped from school was higher than boys.

'1,052 girls dropped from school compared to 84 boys in the second quarter of 2006. This may be attributed to early marriages and other vices,' he said.

He said funding was being channeled to the improvement of schools in the district. He named Katilungu Basic School as one of the beneficiaries of K20 million under the African Development Bank for the construction of three staff houses.

Mungwi Technical school has also been given K300 million for the rehabilitation of dormitories and sanitation by the Government.

Mr Bwembya said insufficient funds to meet the high demands of rehabilitating some educational infrastructure was one of the major challenges in the sector.

Shortage of teachers, especially in distant schools, had also compounded the situation.

Challenges

Inadequate suitable staff and office accommodation has hampered the smooth operations in the district.

Mr Bwembya said most senior government workers were still commuting between Kasama and Mungwi.

He said there was still a problem among the residents that Mungwi was still administered by Kasama.

He also noted that inadequate qualified staff was also another challenge to the district.

Inadequate sector transport system to facilitate the smooth implementation and monitoring of projects in the district to some extent was delaying development.

He said despite the challenges faced, the district with the support from the government and donors was striving to develop.

He said the presence of the Tazara system in the district was a big investment which could attract investors.

The ministry of local Government was also building seven low-cost houses for staff at a cost of K375 million while land for the construction of 100 units of residential houses had been reserved.

The incorporation of the district development plan into the Fifth National Development Plan 2006-2010 was also another milestone.

He appealed to the business community and other stakeholders to take up the responsibility of developing the area.

'I want to appeal to businessmen and women who hail from Mungwi district to invest in Mungwi. There is a lot of potential in fields of agriculture, tourism and mining. The banking sectors are also invited to Mungwi particularly national Savings and Credit Bank (NATSAVE),' he added.

He paid tribute to SIDA, SNV, Cinci Wababili, Justice, Solidarity Poverty Reduction Fund (JSPRF), Irish Aid and Mali investment Zambia Limited (Jatropha Bio-Fuel Company of Kabwe) for helping in the quest to develop the area.

With all these resources, Mungwi promises to be one of the industrial districts not only in the northern province but Zambia at large." – (Anthony Mulowa, "District Status Inspires Mungwi," in *Times of Zambia*, Ndola, Zambia).

Nakonde is the last of the 12 districts in the Northern Province. The district capital is also known as Nakonde.

It's a border district. It borders Tanzania and Malawi. And its capital Nakonde is the border town between Zambia and Tanzania on the Zambian side.

On the other side of the border in Tanzania is the town of Tunduma in Mbozi District. Tunduma has border posts for both the Tanzam Highway – Tanzania-Zambia Highway – and the TAZARA railway for which it has a station.

Until 1997, Nakonde was under the jurisdiction of Isoka District which is about 62 miles away.

When it became a district in 1997, government

departments, private organisations and agencies started opening offices in Nakonde. And with all this came the need for local workers including those with needed skills in different fields.

Many changes have taken place since Nakonde became a district in 1997. But it continues to face challenges in many areas as an underdeveloped district like the rest in the country.

Most people make their living by small-scale farming. Maize and cassava are the staple crops in the area. But few farmers grow enough to feed their families.

Infertile soil, low productivity, the high cost of chemical fertilisers and poor farming methods have contributed to low production.

Ninety-eight percent of Nakonde District has been deforested through land clearance for agriculture, firewood collection and charcoal production, the latter being a major income-generating venture.

Burning wood to make charcoal is a major commercial activity in Nakonde. Charcoal earns a good price on the market, mainly due to demand across the border in Tanzania where fuel wood sources have been depleted.

According to studies made by Zambia's Forest Department, Nakonde District is the second most-deforested district in Zambia after Lusaka.

Charcoal production, firewood collection, and land clearances for agriculture and settlement have not only deforested 98 percent of Nakonde District; they have stunted and even reversed economic growth.

The district also experiences a lot of soil erosion due to heavy rains and lack of trees. Most streams in the district are silted because of lack of ground cover and have water only during the rainy season.

Less than 70 per cent of the people in Nakonde District have access to health facilities or water all year round.

Pregnant women rely on untrained traditional birth attendants to assist them in childbirth, exposing them and their babies to the risk of infection.

HIV/AIDS is second only to malaria as a cause of death among adults; while diarrhoea is the main cause of death in children under five years of age. Malnutrition and skin and eye infections are also common.

But these problems are not peculiar to Nakonde District. They are a national problem, differing only in degree in different parts of the country.

Right next to the Northern Province is the North-Western Province which we are going to look at next.

North-Western Province

The North-Western Province is the most sparsely populated province in the country.

The provincial capital is Solwezi. It's near the border with the Democratic Republic of Congo (DRC). Kaonde is the largest tribe in Solwezi town and district.

The main industry of Solwezi town is copper mining. Gold is also mined. The mining site has been operational since the 1800s.

Three miles from the city centre is the Kifubwa Rock Stream Shelter located next to the Kifubwa River. It has markings, drawings and others symbols, from the late Stone Age.

Like most of Zambia, the North-Western Province is mostly rural. It also has sanctuaries for wildlife including national parks.

The province has seven districts: Chavuma, Kabompo, Kasempa, Mufumbwe, Mwinilunga, Solwezi which we have already looked at, and Zambezi.

The capital of Chavuma District is Chavuma.

The town is located immediately south of the border with Angola. Its attractions include Chavuma Falls. There is also a market on the border with Angola. People from both countries trade and exchange goods there.

Most of the people who live in Chavuma are members of the Luvale tribe.

The people are mostly peasants. They depend on agriculture using simple tools. Many of them are also fishermen.

Chavuma is also known for its cultural festivals. They include Makishi, Mwali and Chilende involving dancing and other festivities of cultural significance to the Luvale people.

All these are strong expressions of ethnic identity and heritage. And they help to sustain the culture – customs and traditions and way of life – of the indigenous people. They also have historical significance in terms of ethnic or tribal origin of the people involved. As Scott D. Taylor states in his book *Culture and Customs of Zambia*:

"Nearly all Zambian ethnic groups can lay claim to a myth of origin and, at some point in their history, celebrated their beginnings.

The Luvale of North-Western Province, for example, hold a festival called Likumbi Lya Mize, or 'the Day of Mize,' which celebrates Mize, the ancient capital of the Luvale people. Held annually in July or August and lasting several days, the Likumbi Lya Mize features the renowned Makishi dancers, the group of young men who wear the elaborate masks known by the same name, which represent key figures in Luvale mythology.

The Makishi dancers also perform at the Mukanda circumcision ceremony...The related Chokwe people have a similar tradition." – (Scott D. Taylor, *Culture and Customs of Zambia*, Santa Barbara, California, USA: Greenwood Press, 2006, p.114).

With relative peace in Angola, there is a lot of cross-border trade at Chavuma between Zambians and Angolans. Chavuma also has an American mission school and hospital built in the 1900s.

Another district in the North-Western Province is Kabompo. The district capital is also known as Kabompo.

The town is located on the Kabompo River. It's surrounded by teak forest.

The town's most significant economic activity is the production of honey.

It's also a town of historical significance in the history and independence struggle of Zambia when the country was still known as Northern Rhodesia.

The town of Kabompo is home to Kabompo House. Kabompo House, No. J11A, Kabompo Township, is a national monument. That's where Kenneth Kaunda, who later became Zambia's first president, was restricted by the colonial authorities from March to July 1959 in an attempt to neutralise his political activities and delay, and if possible, even stop the independence movement.

Kasempa is another district in the North-Western Province.

The district lies to the extreme northwest of Zambia. It's bordered by Congo's Katanga Province in the north, Angola in the west, by Zambia's Barotse and Kafue districts in the south, and Luangwa district in the east.

Its capital is also called Kasempa.

The town is located near the Lufupa and Dongwe Rivers and the Kafue National Park.

Next is Mufumbwe District. It's capital is Mufumbwe. It's located almost in the centre of the district.

Both Kasempa and Mufumbwe have economic potential as mining centres, as do other districts in the region.

Prospects for mining as an important sector of the economy in these districts and in the entire North-Western Province have reshaped the region's landscape in more than one way. According to a report by Zambian journalist Timothy Sichela, "Mining Activities Change North-Western Province's Social Landscape," in the *Times of Zambia*:

"Mining activities at Kansanshi and Lumwana mines in Solwezi have dramatically changed the social landscape of North-Western Province.

And the intensity of the effects of these huge investments, which have come with great potential and challenges, are well-known and documented.

The two large-scale mines are driving the transformation of the once cinderella but otherwise very rich province, creating economic opportunities and providing thousands of jobs, notwithstanding that a good number of these jobs may have been taken by people from outside Solwezi due to low skills levels among locals.

The economic prospects following the re-opening of Kansanshi Mine and the opening of Lumwana Mine have come with great possibilities to impact lives of the local people. And these perceived opportunities have attracted droves from other parts of Zambia.

And as a result of the migration, there is much strain on social and other basic services including health, education, housing as well as recreational facilities. Infrastructure developed for a small population is struggling to cope, and implications include illegal structures emerging.

With the former ZCCM mines having demonstrated a steadfast support to communities in towns they operated on the Copperbelt, maintaining roads, providing medical, educational, sporting and other recreational facilities, the people of Solwezi are enthusiastic about the mines.

Kansanshi public relations manager, Godfrey Msiska, whose company has spent millions of Kwacha on projects in Solwezi under its Kansanshi Foundation, says: 'The Kansanshi Mining Plc philosophy is to enrich the environment and communities in which we operate. This is in line with the First Quantum Minerals (FQM) group ethos of adding value to the communities in which it operates.'

Equinox Minerals, who have built a mine and township on a former greenfield in Lumwana, and FQM group, owners of Kansanshi Mine, are striving to make a difference as corporate social citizens of Solwezi. But even after pumping billions on community projects in their support for Government efforts in providing health and education services, the two mines still appear under pressure from the locals to take more responsibility for social and economic impacts in communities affected by their operations.

To somewhat explain why the investors seem to continue receiving the flak, a researcher, Kinsley Cheelo puts it aptly in his paper 'behind the economic figures: large- scale mining and rural poverty reduction in Zambia. The case of Kansanshi Mine':

'One could argue that local communities benefit from investors' presence through their corporate social responsibilities, but the fact that investors are not welfare organisations and are not experts in service delivery implies that even under this initiative the locals still lose out.'

But it's not all locals complaining. Solwezi-Kansanshi Lions Club president, Elisha Zgambo and other many beneficiary organisations like Youth Alive Zambia applaud Kansanshi that despite the global economic meltdown, the mine had continued to contribute to the social and economic well being of communities in which it operates.

'This in the essence of humanity bears a reflection of the mine being a concerned investment geared to change the image of the community through its corporate social responsibility (CSR) programme,' Mr Zgambo said recently after Kansanshi gave his organisation K10 million for community projects.

And with the mining companies appearing under unrelenting pressure to do more, the Catholic Diocese of Solwezi conducted a survey to get specific information on the social, economic or environmental impacts of mining

118

activities on surrounding communities in the province.

The study, which investigated the corporate social responsibility agenda of the mines in the province, revealed that while Kansanshi and Lumwana had CSR strategies, the corporate social responsibility was a missing virtue in mining activities in Kasempa and Mufumbwe.

Researcher Stephen Muyakwa, releasing findings of a recent baseline study on CSR for the Catholic Diocese of Solwezi through its Zambia Extractive Industries Project, said community responses in Solwezi confirmed contrasting approaches of Kansanshi and Lumwana mines.

'Kansanshi has shown to have a traditional approach to CSR of giving away money and projects as and when the management feels it is time to make a gesture of goodwill or as a form of philanthropy.

Lumwana, on the other hand, has shown to have built-in the CSR policies, strategies and has in place structures to consult with local communities on priorities and concerns of local people. Lumwana has, thus a modern approach to CSR,' Mr Muyakwa said.

The study found that the situation in the other mining districts of the province Kasempa, Mufumbwe and, to a limited extent Mwinilunga, was different but more critical than Solwezi.

'Mining activities in Kasempa and Mufumbwe are mostly characterised by small-scale quasi-legal mining operations with no CSR policies. The situation is particularly worrying in Kasempa where illegal mining operators have set up camp in various parts of the game management areas combining mining with tourism activities,' he said.

He said the research found that North-Western Province was poised to join the ranks of major copper and other mineral producing and exporting regions of Zambia and the world.

'This is a big development as it brings with it big risks

but more importantly, big opportunities. This study has shown that the country has had a long history of copper mining and has over the years put in place policies to manage the mining sector," Mr Muyakwa said.

And on policies and regulations, the survey found that Zambia had important documents like the Vision 2030, Fifth National Development Plan and laws like the Mines and Minerals Development Act 2008, environmental protection regulations and indeed, labour regulations.

'The study has further shown that there are some weaknesses in the policies and regulations, in particular the absence of the all important empowering clause in the Constitution and the mining law providing for legal rights to community ownership of mineral resources within their areas,' he said.

He said the research showed serious social conditions of poverty, HIV/ AIDS, health and educational deprivation existing in the province, contrasting with the vast economic potential existing in the province for the production of various agricultural products such as mixed beans, cattle and honey.

'It is hoped that the baseline data presented will form the core set of indicators for measuring the impacts of the mining sector on social, economic and cross cutting variables of gender and environment,' he said.

Among the strategies the study recommended to the Government was the inclusion of a clause in the Constitution providing legal ownership of mining and other resources to the local people and ensure that some of the revenues from mining activities went to the community through improvements in schools, health facilities and economic infrastructure.

To civil society organisations (CSO), the research suggested among other strategies to monitor and acknowledge the efforts of different mining companies and devise a scheme of rewarding the best and worst performing mining companies in terms of CSR policy and practice.

And to the cooperating partners, it recommended that they assist in building the capacity of CSOs, local communities and the Government in ensuring that pro-poor economic policies were formulated, implemented and monitored.

Hoping that the growth of the mining industry in the province would answer the aspiration of the people, Catholic Diocese of Solwezi, vicar-general Albert Sakala said the study intended to call for public policy, law or programme change aimed at poverty reduction.

'When we look at the recent growth in the mining sector in Zambia and the opportunities it presents to the local communities, there is a ready source for comparison. The growth of the industry should answer the aspiration of the Zambian people, in particular those of the North-Western Province,' Fr Sakala said.

He said with billions of dollars invested in the mining projects, a lot of development was taking place in North-Western Province, and the mining industry had brought with it much hope and aspirations to the people in the province and Zambia in general.

Diocesan Caritas coordinator, Frederick Nabanda said the civil society were not against investors and the Government but were actually looking for the best way for a common approach to solving people's problems and improving their standards of living.

Mr Nabanda said lack of previous information on the impact of extractive industries on communities in the province impeded Solwezi Diocese's capacity to effectively design and subsequently evaluate activities aimed at empowering communities socially, economically and environmentally.

'As part of the Zambia Extractive Industries Project, the Catholic Diocese of Solwezi is undertaking a number of activities aimed at gathering information to strengthen national and international advocacy efforts and to empower local communities to understand and monitor the industry's impact, and in turn, advocate on their own behalf locally,' he said." – (Timothy Sichela, "Mining Activities Change North-Western Province's Social Landscape," in *Times of Zambia*, Ndola, Zambia, 11 August 2009).

Mwinilunga is another district in the North-Western Province. It's on the West Lunga River close to the borders with the Democratic Republic of Congo (DRC) and Angola.

The district capital is also called Mwinilunga.

Located almost at the northwestern tip of the district in an area bordering Congo, the town has the distinction of being one of the wettest places in Zambia during the rainy season from October to May.

The Chilunda-speaking Kanongesha-Lunda people are the largest ethnic group in the town and in the district. They're related to the Chimbemba-speaking Kazembe-Lunda of Luapula Province.

Attempts were made to establish industries in the town of Mwinilunga. They included the TIKA Iron and Steel plant and a pineapple cannery. But the industries were not commercially successful and had to be closed down because of the long distance from Mwinilunga to the markets of the Copperbelt and the lack of a railway and source of coking coal for the iron and steel plant.

There were also plans in 2006 to extend the railway which goes to Solwezi so that it can reach Mwinilunga. An extension was also proposed to connect with the Benguela Railway in Angola to avoid reliance on the line in neighbouring Congo. But none of these plans had been implemented in 2010 and the Benguela Railway had not been re-opened by then.

Mwinilunga can benefit from trade with Angola and Congo, reinforced by ethnic ties since both countries have large numbers of the Lunda people like Zambia including those in Mwinilunga. But wars, poor road conditions and unfavourable trade policies have made it almost impossible for commercial ties to be established among these neighbouring countries in that part of the North-Western Province.

Forest Fruits Ltd. has been operating in Mwinilunga since 1997, successfully working with over 5000 beekeepers in the region to export organic honey to the European market.

The area is also rich in mineral deposits, especially copper and uranium. And mines for these minerals already exist in different parts along the highway between Solwezi and Mwinilunga.

The annual *Chisemwa Cha Lunda* ceremony held by the senior chief of the Lunda people draws large crowds to Mwinilunga District every September.

The annual ceremony is held at the end of the dry season to welcome the rainy season.

The last district in the North-Western Province is Zambezi. Its capital or district headquarters is also called Zambezi located in the western part of the district which looks like a panhandle.

The town of Zambezi is on the Zambezi River. It's known for the residences of the chiefs of the Balunda and the Balovale tribes.

Until about 1966, the town was called Balovale, named after the dominant chief. His village within the town is still known by that name.

The town's name was changed in an attempt to defuse tensions between the main ethnic groups – the Lunda and the Lovale – and the government of the new nation of Zambia.

Next we look at the Southern Province.

Southern Province

The Southern Province stands out among all the provinces in Zambia for two reasons.

It's home to the world-famous Victoria Falls, one of the biggest tourist attractions on the entire continent and in the world. The Falls are shared with Zimbabwe.

The Southern Province also has the largest area of commercial farmland in Zambia, an area that also produces most of the maize in the country. This fertile area is in the centre of the province and is known as the Southern Plateau.

In addition to maize, other commercially important activities in the province include sugarcane plantations and cattle ranching.

The Zambezi River is the province's southern border, and Lake Kariba, formed by Kariba Dam, lies along the southeastern part of the province.

The southwestern border with the Western Province runs through the teak forests around Mulobezi which once supported a commercial timber industry and for which the Mulobezi Railway was built.

Although Mulobezi is a small town, it's the centre of the timber industry in the Southern Province. Located on the border with the Western Province in the southwestern part of the Southern Province, Mulobezi is virtually synonymous with "timber" in Zambia.

The capital of the Southern Province is Livingstone.

The Batonga, also known as Tonga, are the largest ethnic group in the Southern Province.

A railway and the Lusaka-Livingstone Road forms the main transport axis of the province, running through its centre and its farming towns of Kalomo, Choma, Pemba, Monze, and Mazabuka.

The Southern Province has the only large source of fossil fuel in Zambia, the Maamba coal mine in the Zambezi valley, served by a railway branch line.

In addition to Victoria Falls, the Southern Province has other major tourist attractions including national parks and other animal sanctuaries.

The Southern Province has 11 districts: Choma, Gwembe, Itezhi-Tezhi, Kalomo, Kazungula, Livingstone, Mazabuka, Monze, Namwala, Siavonga, and Sinazongwe.

As with all the other districts, the district headquarters, which are mostly small towns except in a few cases, are the centres of political activities and major events in the districts.

We are going to look at them here as we have done with all the other districts in the provinces we have covered so far.

Choma, the capital of Choma District, is a market town located on the main road and railway from Lusaka to Livingstone. It's almost in the centre of the district.

The town has a small museum dedicated to the cultural heritage of the Tonga people who constitute the largest ethnic groups in southern Zambia.

And besides being the district headquarters of Choma District, the town also serves as the commercial hub for the central region of the province.

The district has the typical climate of southern Zambia with temperatures between 57°F and 82°F.

After Choma, the next district we're going to look at is Gwembe.

The former capital of Gwembe District is Gwembe. It's a small town with only about 2,000 people. But it's the largest town in the district.

The district headquarters was moved to Munyumbwe about 18-and-a-half miles east of Gwembe.

One of the main agricultural activities in Gwembe District is cotton growing. And the town of Gwembe has a cotton ginnery plant which provides employment to the town's residents and others nearby.

Itezhi-Tezhi is another district in the Southern province. Its capital is also named Itezhi-Tezhi.

It's a small town west of Namwala, the capital of neighbouring Namwala District.

The town of Itezhi-Tezhi owes its existence to the construction of Itezhi-Tezhi Dam on the Kafue River in the early 1970's. The dam was created to hold and regulate the water flow in the river for Kafue Gorge Power Station lower downstream.

The town's population was estimated to be 4,000 people in 2010. And the main employer in the town is the Zambian Electricity Supply Company (ZESCO).

Next we look at Kalomo, the capital of Kalomo District.

Located almost in the centre of the district, the town of Kalomo is on the main road and railway line to Lusaka.

And it played a very important role in the history of the country when it was a British colony.

Kalomo was the first administrative centre of Northern Rhodesia. It served as the colony's administrative centre until 1911 when the capital was moved to Livingstone. The Administrator's House in Kalomo still exists as a reminder of that era. The house was the residence of the governor of Northern Rhodesia.

The area has another historical significance. There is a a site near the town of Kalomo which is more than 1,000 years old. The site is known as Kalundu Mound. It's the site of a village from at least the 9th century. The village lasted until the 12th century.

Another town in the Southern Province is Kazungula, the capital of Kazungula District.

It's a small border town located on the northern bank of the Zambezi River about 43-and-a-half miles west of Livingstone at a point where four countries meet: Zambia, Zimbabwe, Botswana, and Namibia.

Botswana has only about one mile of river frontage on

the Zambezi. It's sandwiched on the southern bank between the extreme tip of Namibia's Caprivi Strip and Zimbabwe. This is th meeting point of the four countries.

Kazungula is also home to the Kazungula Ferry which carries cargo and passengers across the Zambezi to the town of Kasane in Botswana. The ferry is one of the largest in the region.

Kazungula is about a mile from the Livingstone-Sesheke road which goes to the Katima Mulilo Bridge linking Zambia and Namibia.

The Chobe River which divides Namibia and Botswana flows into the Zambezi at Kazungula.

The Zimbabwe border post which is almost 3 miles – by road – southeast of the Kazungula Ferry is also called Kazungula.

The largest urban centre in the Southern Province is Livingstone which is the provincial capital. It's also the capital of Livingstone District.

But we're not going to look at this city in this part of the book. It's covered in the next part which deals with the main towns and cities of Zambia.

We now look at Mazabuka, the capital of Mazabuka District in the Southern Province.

The town is located southwest of Lusaka on the main road and railway to Livingstone.

The town of Mazabuka has grown around sugarcane plantations. One of these plantations is the famous Nakambala Estate.

Monze is another district in the Southern Province. The district headquarters is also named Monze. It's located about 112 miles southwest of Lusaka, the nation's capital.

The town of Monze is named after Chief Monze, widely acknowledged as the spiritual leader of the Tonga people who inhabit the district.

His palace is located south of the town near a place called Gonde where a ceremony called Lwiindi takes place. This annual festival is a thanksgiving ceremony which attracts a lot of people from around the country.

The traditional ceremony usually takes place during the first week of July, coinciding with the country's Heroes and Unity holidays which are also celebrated in the same week.

The main economic activity in Monze District is farming. Maize is the most important crop.

At one point in the past, the district used to produce more than 25 per cent of the maize crop in Zambia. During that period, it was popularly known as the "home of Zambia's granary."

Although its status as the leading maize producer in Zambia has declined over the years, the most prominent feature in the town is still the grain silos to the north of the town.

Next we go to Namwala. It's a rural district like most of the districts in the country. Its capital is also known as Namwala.

Other major settlement areas or townships or village-towns in Namwala District are Kabulamwanda, Muchila, Maala, Mbeza and Chitongo.

The town of Namwala lies on the southern bank of the Kafue River. It's also the main town of the members of the Ila ethnic group. The Ila, also known as Ba-Ila, are native inhabitants of the district.

They're famous for their large herds of cattle. Their main economic activity is livestock farming.

The Ila people engage mostly in cattle herding, fishing, hunting and subsistence farming.

As a symbol of prestige, the traditional Ila simply keep their cattle. They do not routinely eat cow meat. But drought and disease have taken a toll on the cattle population.

The Ila are closely related in language and culture to their more numerous Tonga neighbours who also live in the Southern Province.

The Ila live mainly in the districts of Namwala, Itezhi-

Tezhi and Mumbwa. They're spread over seventeen chiefdoms.

Namwala District is also well known for its traditional ceremony known as Shimunenga. This spectacular event takes place every year at Maala village.

Shimunenga is considered by the Ila people of Maala to be a divine being. They believe they have to pray to him when the crops need blessing, the cattle are to be taken to the plains, or when a murder is committed.

The ceremony is an occasion for the people to thank their god for providing for them over the period which has just passed.

The ceremony takes place once a year between September and November at the close of the old year and the beginning of the new one. It lasts for 3 days and takes place at the homes of the Ba-ila of Maala.

Early in the morning of the first day, people gather at the shrine of Shimunenga where traditional songs are sung. There is also a cultural march past of women and girls in traditional attire, after which the people enjoy spectacular performances by traditional dancers.

On the following morning, the drum is sounded and animals are taken to the river where cattle are displayed in the traditional manner.

The first cattle to cross the river will be those of the custodian of the shrine.

This traditional event is followed by a demonstration of a mock lion hunt and pelican fishing.

The occasion is marked with traditional songs in honour and praise of the Shimunenga ancestral spirits.

Celebrations continue in the village with pit-stops for traditional beer at different places.

Another district in the Southern Province is Siavonga whose capital also is known as Siavonga.

The town is located on the northern shore of Lake Kariba. It's Zambia's main tourism centre for the lake, providing accommodation, boating and fishing tours, among other things.

The last district in the Southern Province is Sinazongwe. Its capital is also called Sinazongwe.

A small town on the northern shore of Lake Kariba, Sinazongwe was built in the 1950s as a local administrative centre. Its main industry is *kapenta* fishing. Ferries also travel from Sinazongwe to Chete Island.

Chete Island is in Lake Kariba. It's a bird sanctuary and home to other forms of wildlife. There are other smaller islands in the lake.

The animals on the islands have been virtually undisturbed since the Kariba Dam was built in the 1950s. They were trapped on the islands when the water rose after the dam was built and they have been there ever since.

Animals on Chete Island include elephants, lions and leopards. Apart from being an animal sanctuary, Chete Island is also a tourist destination, and an important part of the economy of the area which includes Sinazongwe.

Sinazongwe is a fast-developing area in Zambia. Commercial plots have been sold to potential investors. Many of the investors are in the tourism sector.

Sinazongwe is accessible nearly all year round.

Sinazongwe is also the first place that travellers from South Africa, Namibia and Botswana can get to see or visit Lake Kariba.

In terms of tourism, Sinazongwe is relatively untouched, with little external influence and commercial activity. But there are various local traditional ceremonies including the Lwiindi ceremony in July-August which tourists attend.

Lwiindi is an annual ceremony of the Tonga people, a festival of thanks to the ancestors for rain and good harvest.

In fact, among all the tribes, the Tonga are believed to have lived the longest in the area that came to be known as Northern Rhodesia and later Zambia. It's believed they have lived in the Tonga area in the Southern Province for

600 years.

Evidence of their stay here have been found in places such as Mazabuka, Magoye, Monze, Choma, Kalomo, Batoka plateau and at the top of Sebanzi hill on the edge of the Kafue flats on Lochinvar ranch.

Tonga is a Shona word meaning independent. The name indicates that the Tonga people did not have a central political structure. They lived in small independent family units.

The Tonga people are very much attached to their land and cattle. Members of other Zambian tribes often tease them saying, when you greet a Tonga, you must also enquire about the wellbeing of each and very cow.

The Lwiindi traditional ceremony encompasses several ceremonies; all of them are connected to praying for rain. The main ones are the Lwiindi Gonde held southwest of Monze town, and the Maanzi Aabila Lwiindi, in Chief Siachitima's area in Kalomo. They are held annually.

Shrines are also an integral part of Tonga culture. The shrines are located at Gonde, which means thick bush. The Tonga visit the shrines to ask for rain from their ancestors or assistance with eliminating disease.

At the shrines there are two huts built on top of the graves of the sacred Tonga chiefs – Mayaba and Nchete Ilya Mabwe. When praying for rain, the Tonga brew beer, slaughter a black goat or chicken or even a cow.

There are strict rules the people must follow when they're at the shrines.

Women are not allowed if they're in their menstrual period.

An animal slaughtered at the shrine must be roasted and eaten without adding salt. And the meat must be eaten right there at the shrine.

The people must remove their shoes and socks.

Any person going to the shrines must be clean of mind and body.

You should not have sex the night before going to the

shrine.

Those are just some of the rules.

The Lwiindi ceremony is the main ceremony which takes place in July. The ceremony is held at Gonde where it's claimed the first Chief Monze just disappeared but did not die. Chief Monze is considered to be the most senior leader of the Tonga.

Gonde became the burial place for all chiefs but so far only two have been buried there.

Lwiindi means thanksgiving for the harvests. The thanks are directed to Tonga ancestors, especially the first Chief, Monze Mukulukulu. It's believed that Monze Mukulukulu was blessed with wisdom, was a rain maker and could eradicate diseases.

The Tonga people would travel long distances to come and seek his advice. Before they spoke to him, they would present him with traditional hoes – *maamba* – made from smelted iron.

Chief Monze celebrates the Lwiindi Gonde ceremony by consuming the first meal of the new season's harvest. In the process, songs are sung praising the first Chief Monze Mukulukulu who, according to tradition, sends down the rain.

The ceremony attracts many people including politicians and others from different parts of Zambia beyond the province. It's not just for the people of the Southern Province who attend the festival.

In July 2009, the president of Tanzania, Jakaya Kikwete, also attended the ceremony. According to a report, "'Tongas Are Very Peaceful and Hardworking,'" in *Lusaka Times*:

"Presidents Rupiah Banda and his Tanzanian counterpart, Jakaya Kikwete, were yesterday among hundreds of people who turned out to celebrate this year's Lwiindi traditional ceremony in Chief Monze's area.

Speaking when he officially opened the Lwiindi

traditional ceremony, President Banda said Tongas were very peaceful and hardworking people.

Mr Banda called on all Zambians to remain united, adding that this was the only way the country could achieve economic development in both the education and health sectors.

He urged Zambians to remain united and listen to the advice offered by their leaders.

Mr Banda also thanked Tanzanian President, Mr Kikwete, for having accepted to attend the Lwiidi ceremony at short notice.

And speaking earlier, Mr Kikwete urged the Tonga people to preserve and guard their culture and commended Chief Monze for preserving the Tonga culture in the age of Information, Communication Technology (ICT) and the global village.

Mr Kikwete said maintaining the traditional culture was a big challenge in the age of computers, television sets and other gadgets such as cellular phones, that seemed to be stealing the hearts of young people.

'Our young people tend to spend more time on these gadgets and in the process learn and acquire foreign culture which leads to the degrading of our traditional African culture,' he said.

He said there was a need to be vigilant if the traditional culture was to be maintained.

'Please maintain these important traditions. Make sure that the younger people and the educated men and women are fully involved and participate in these traditional ceremonies and ensure that they do not participate like expatriates from Europe,' he said.

He noted that Africans must be proud to participate in their own culture whether they were educated or not.

Mr Kikwete described his participation at this year's Lwiindi traditional ceremony as revolutionary because Heads of States ended in other countries' capital cities and rarely in the villages.

'Taking a visiting Head of State to a village to witness a traditional ceremony is something that President Banda deserves applaud. Thank you Chief Monze for agreeing with President Banda and allowing me to witness this ceremony of the Tonga people dedicated to thanking God for the good rains and harvest. I am very impressed with what I have seen,' he said.

And Chief Monze thanked both Presidents Banda and Kikwete for agreeing to grace this year's Lwiindi ceremony.

He said his desire was to see a ceremony that was not only peaceful but also non-political, adding that this was the reason why he had directed everybody going to attend the ceremony not to put on any clothing with political inclination.

Chief Monze also appealed to government to recognise him as Paramount Chief of the Tonga people in Southern Province.

'I'm the 9th Paramount Chief. I ask government to recognise me as Paramount Chief in this province.'

Chief Monze also appealed to his people to work hard and uplift the country in terms of agriculture.

Patron of the Lwiindi Tradition ceremony, Hakainde Hichilema, said collectively, Zambia could address the challenges the country was facing.

And chairman of the Lwiindi traditional ceremony, Rex Matala, urged government to closely monitor the distribution of fertilser under the Agriculture Support Programme (FSP).

He said the coming of two Heads of State to address the ceremony was historical, adding that as long as he remained chairman of the traditional ceremony, he would ensure that the event was not politicized.

Mr Matala further said that traditional ceremonies were not places to show political strength, but were meant to bring people together in unity.

President Rupiah Banda and his counterpart Mr

Kikwete have since flown back to Livingstone where they are expected to attend another ceremony that will be held at Chief Mukuni's palace in Kazungula district." – ("'Tongas Are Very Peaceful and Hardworking,'" in *Lusaka Times*, Lusaka, Zambia, 7 July 2009).

A similar report, "Rupiah Calls for Unity Among Zambians," about the ceremony was also published in the *Times of Zambia*:

"President Rupiah Banda has called for unity among Zambians to achieve economic development for all.

Mr Banda was speaking in Monze during the Lwiindi Gonde traditional ceremony of the Tonga people yesterday.

The ceremony was also attended by Tanzanian President, Jakaya Kikwete and opposition United Party for National Development leader, Hakainde Hichilema, who is also patron of the Lwiindi Gonde traditional ceremony.

There were also ministers, deputy ministers, members of Parliament, diplomats and representatives from the private sector.

Paramount Chief Mpezeni, Chief Sandwe and Chief Chikanta were among the traditional leaders who witnessed this year's Lwiindi Gonde traditional ceremony.

Mr Banda said the Tonga people of Southern Province were a united tribe where hard work was at the centre of the development being experienced in the area.

He said the Tonga people were generous.

'I wish prosperity for our people, our children and for the good delivery of services such as health to the people.

'However, this can only be achieved if we remain united as our forefathers left us,' he said.

He urged Zambians to listen to their leaders because the country has to remain united.

And Mr Kikwete hailed Senior Chief Moonze for maintaining tradition and culture in Zambia.

Mr Kikwete said maintaining culture and tradition was a major challenge in this age of increasing information and communication technologies where young people were adopting foreign lifestyles.

'I am very impressed with what I have seen and heard here, especially from Chief Moonze who has managed to uphold and preserve culture and tradition in this area.

'To maintain African tradition and culture is a big challenge, especially with the advent of information communication technologies such as televisions, mobile phones, video games and computers, which have been stealing the minds of the young people,' he said.

Mr Kikwete said young people in Africa spent more time on the electronic gadgets and were acquiring foreign cultures and traditions which contributed to the decay of culture.

President Kikwete said Zambians must guard against moral decay.

'I am happy to be here because this event is all about maintaining important traditions, but we must ensure that the youth and educated young men and women are fully involved and they should participate actively and not do so like expatriates from Europe,' he said.

Mr Kikwete said the Lwiindi traditional ceremony was an important event because it was about thanking God for the good rain and good harvests.

'I am with you in thanking and asking God for good harvests and good rain. There should be no season where there is no rain, and may the good harvests continue until judgement day,' he said.

Earlier, Lwiidi Gonde chairperson, Rex Natala said the traditional ceremony must not be turned into a political battle ground where politicians should showcase their political muscle.

'I will make sure that this traditional ceremony is not politicised by the ruling party or the opposition. This is not a place where you can show your political strength. We want to be good citizens and this is not a place for drunkenness or prostitution,' he said.

Mr Natala said Senior Chief Moonze was a serious man who did not want to see moral decay in his chiefdom.

He said the Government had shown commitment to traditional ceremonies and economic development for Zambians.

'The Government policies show a commitment to fighting poverty, but we would like to urge the Government to implement the policies effectively for the benefit of the people,' he said.

Mr Natala cited the Fertiliser Support Programme where he said the initiative must benefit the poor unlike now where unscrupulous businessmen and other traders have hijacked the project.

'Our farmers had a good harvest in crops such as sweet potatoes but there is no market to sell these commodities,' he said.

Senior Chief Moonze said people who wanted to saturate the traditional norms in his chiefdom by dressing inappropriately should leave their attire outside because he would not allow immorality.

Mr Hichilema said the Lwiindi traditional ceremony was not about celebrating war.

He said the ceremony was about development among the Tonga people.

'This ceremony is about thanking God for the good harvest and asking for good rain,' he said." – (Richard Mulonga and Edward Mulenga, "Rupiah Calls for Unity Among Zambians," in the *Times of Zambia*, Ndola, Zambia, 7 July 2009).

The ceremony starts on the last Sunday of June. On Sunday, people watch various dances of the plateau Tonga, the plains Tonga and the valley Tonga.

The plateau Tonga perform the Kalyaba dance using only two drums. This is a spiritual dance that moves the soul and mind.

The valley Tonga perform a warrior dance known as Budima. This is the song that brings the chief into the main arena. The performance is also called Nyeele and is also used to drive cattle into the bush.

The Budima dance is performed by traditional soldiers with long spears, jumping high while blowing trumpet music and shouting chants, while a big drum sounds from the corner of the arena.

There is also a dance performed by old women and young girls adorned with bead necklaces and bangles of white beads on their arms. It's an energetic dance which includes older mentor women. It's performed at initiation ceremonies for girls getting ready to be married.

And it's all about true Tonga identity, ethnic, cultural and spiritual, also in the larger context as an integral part of the nation that is indivisible.

Western Province

Finally, we look at the Western Province, what's also known as Barotseland, inhabited by the Barotse, commonly known as the Lozi, one of the largest and most well-known ethnic groups in Zambia with a long history of independence under their traditional ruler or king.

The name Barotseland was used especially during the colonial era but it's still identified with this province whose inhabitants were opposed to a centralised form of government under a unitary state. Their dissatisfaction with central authority and demands for autonomy threatened national unity during the first years of independence.

There were, in fact very strong separatist tendencies in Barotseland before and after the end of colonial rule especially during the first years of independence.

The geography of the province is dominated by the

Barotse Floodplain of the Zambezi River.

The floodplain – which can be up to 75 miles wide – is inundated from December to June, and is fed by other rivers with their own floodplains, and serves as a vast reservouir storing the waters of the Zambezi River.

The seasonal flooding is very important to agriculture in the province, providing natural irrigation for the grasslands on which huge herds of cattle depend. It also brings water to the settlements along the edges of the plain.

The capital of the Western Province is Mongu. But it's not well-supplied with paved roads.

The main road and access to the province is the 379-mile road from Lusaka to Mongu which is also known as the Great West Road.

The Lozi, who are the major ethnic group in the province, are traditionally cattle-keepers. They are a collection of 24 subgroups with a well-established system of traditional rulers headed by the Litunga, a title equivalent to king.

The Litunga is assisted by subchiefs in Sesheke Senanga and Kalabo.

The seasonal migrations – *kuomboka* - of the Litunga and his court from the dry-season capital of Leauli on the Zambezi flood-plain to Limulunga is not only an important cultural event; it's also very important for tourism. Many people from outside the province and from other countries witness the event.

There is an ethnic minority group of the Nkoya people in Kaoma District who live under their own traditional rulers. The Nkoya are not part of the political system administered by the Lozi king.

The Nkoya are, together with the Tonga of the Southern Province, one of the oldest groups in Zambia. They have lived in what later came to be known as Zambia for hundreds of years.

Their language has 12 dialects spread across many

provinces: Western, North-Western, Central, Lusaka and Southern provinces.

The dialects include Lukolwe, Mashasha, Lushangi, Nkoya Shasha Mbowela, and Lumbu.

The Nkoya also celebrate their annual traditional ceremony called the Kazanga or Kathanga between June and August in Kaoma District. As Zambian journalist Kennedy Limwanya stated in his report, "Kathanga Ceremony: Nkoyas Assert Themselves," in the *Times of Zambia*:

"The Kathanga ceremony, according to a great grandson of a Nkoya chief, Kangombe, has galvanised the Nkoyas and established them as one of the major tribal groupings in Zambia.

Robert Litungu, grandson of Kangombe, a Nkoya chieftain, explains that the ceremony was discontinued during colonial rule because its ethno-cultural value was not understood.

'And yet the Nkoya, like the other African societies in East and Central Africa, had a proud and strong belief in their traditional myths and deities which they often associated with their pre-colonial origins,' Mr Litungu says.

The ceremony was, however, revived in 1988 and was held at the then reigning Mwene (chief) Mutondo Muchaila's Lukena palace in Kaoma (previously Mankoya) and today celebrates its 13th year of 're-birth.'

Historically, the Kathanga, which has been held since the founding of the Nkoya state, was a traditional rite performed as a thanksgiving event to God (Nyambi) for a bumper harvest.

It was also a military occasion to honour gallant Nkoya tribesmen and warriors who had performed heroic exploits like fighting other tribes and killing marauding animals such as lions and leopards.

The ceremony involved a continuous beating of a

140

special drum, drinking sweet beer made from fresh sorghum known as muzinge which was poured into the kabangula, a small hole dug in the ground near the Kaala-Shihanda ancestral shrine.

In the distant past, the kabangula, a drinking cup, was made from the upper part of a human skull, usually of a dead enemy, to emphasis sacred ritual associated with the enemy.

At the Kaala-Shihanda shrine, Nkoya chiefs and heroes were anointed and smeared with mpemba, a lump of white clay, to signify a blessing by the ancestral spirits and the tribal god.

This shrine was, and still is, the place where the installation ceremony of new chiefs was performed.

The ceremony, however, has now been demystified and is today attended by not only Nkoyas but other tribes, Government leaders and tourists who have continued to add colour since its revival in 1988.

Much has been done to change the face of the ceremony which is this year taking place today and tomorrow at Shinchoncho, a place which was chosen for logistical convenience.

It lies on the banks of the Luena river, 15 kilometres east of Kaoma which makes it easy for visitors to find accommodation as it is near town.

With the changing times, the objectives of the ceremony have also been steadily changing and now appear to have taken a new direction.

'The major objective now is the provision of entertainment and leisure through music. There's also the passing on of tradition. We also have accomplished drummers mixing with young people hence imparting their knowledge into the youngsters,' says Mr Litungu.

He picks upon the year 2000 as the most successful since the revival of the ceremony as evidenced by the heavy presence of many Nkoya chiefs and traditional leaders of other tribes.

'Last year the ceremony was attended by nearly all Nkoya chiefs. From Kabombo came chiefs Mutinginyi and Kangombe, there was Kabulwebulwe from Mumbwa and Moomba from Kazungula. That was besides the two Nkoya-based chiefs Mutondo and Kahare.'

According to Mr Litungu, the Kathanga ceremony has achieved some of the objectives that were set out in 1988 and quite creditable successes have been recorded.

'Previously, people never knew about the Nkoya, especially the musical repertoire like the shilimba and the munkupele which were mistaken for Lozi music,' explains Mr Litungu who has just finished a manuscript on the ceremony and the Nkoya traditions and customs.

He adds that the ceremony now involves not only villages but also the Nkoyas 'from the diaspora' or urban areas who go back to the village to go and acquaint themselves with the Nkoya history.

The origins of the Nkoya, as derived from Mr Litungu's writing, are incoherent mainly because they came into what is now Zambia a long time ago, about 1700 AD.

But, he continues, according to Nkoya oral sources, their migration into Zambia from what is now Zaire was led by a female ruler Lbupe, a Luba, from an area around the Lualaba river before the rise of the Luba-Lunda kingdom of Mwatiamvwa.

The Nkoya are today settled on the Luena river and its tributaries such as the Luampa river together with its middle sections to the west and on the Lalafuta river to the east.

Others are settled on the lower Kabompo river and its tributaries mainly on the Dongwe and its tributaries.

Since the re-birth of the Kathanga, many Nkoya people have played a leading role in ensuring that it comes to what it is today.

These are people like Messrs Robert Kakundu and John Maini of Ndola, William Shihenya, Stanford

Mayowe, Reverend Mowat Kambita, the late James Kalaluka and Litungu himself.

But the annual holding of the ceremony has not been without its own difficulties, particularly with the effects of the biting economy and, in Mr Litungu's words, the little recognition of Nkoyas in key national positions.

'Initially, our aim was to make the event self-sustaining. But the prevailing circumstances have made it extremely difficult to raise funds for the provision of food for invited guests and visiting dignitaries,' laments Mr Litungu.

The yearly budget, he adds, is never met in full and this year has not been an exception although there have been well-wishers like Dar Farms International and other transporters.

Another problem has been the relaxed stance taken by some Nkoyas outside Lusaka although Mr Litungu observes that retrenchments and deaths of key organisers could be another factor.

Although the Kathanga Cultural Association led by Edwin Nkhomesha has received some support from President Chiluba as an individual and the Government in general, much needs to be done.

Other influential members of the association have been Fredah Luhila who is the secretary and treasurer Webster Mulubisha.

'President Chiluba has been supportive. Some time back he met our chiefs and provided financial support. Our appeal to the Government is to continue assisting the ceremony through the royal establishments to ensure that the Nkoya culture is preserved for posterity.'

This year's ceremony at which Community Development minister Jane Chikwata is expected to officiate, should provide visitors with such traditional dances as makwasha, ntomboke, lunhwa and kamunyelele.

Mr Litungu admits that it is not easy to promote culture especially with the on-rush of western culture but conditions can be created for co-existence.

'It's difficult to completely go back to the old traditions, but like in any society, there are people who are wary. We can always co-exist. For instance, the Masai culture in East Africa has attained international status. There's also the reed ceremony in Swaziland. With Government support, we can do it.'

On the performance of the Kathanga Cultural Association, Mr Litungu says much has been done, given the harsh economic conditions.

'We've done very well. The tribe is not so economically empowered. Many of our people don't go to school and although hard-working, we are timid and docile hence allowing ourselves to be overrun,' he explains.

Indeed, it is said a nation without culture is a dead nation." – (Kennedy Limwanya, "Kathanga Ceremony: Nkoyas Assert Themselves," in *Times of* Zambia, Ndola, Zambia, 12 June 2004).

Although western Zambia is known as the land of the Lozi, there are other ethnic groups in the Western Province, for example, the Nkoya we have just looked at. But the Lozi are still the dominant group in the province. They're also one of the most powerful in Zambia.

Cattle are the mainstay of the traditional economy in the Western Province. They're sold when money is required for cash goods or for school, medical and other expenses.

Crops grown on the floodplains and along the margin of the flood plain include maize, rice, millet and vegetables.

Logging for Zambian teak, which grows wild in the southern part of the province, was once very important and resulted in the construction of the longest private railway in southern Africa from Livingstone to Mulobezi.

But the teak industry has declined due to very slow rates of re-growth and reduced demand for railway sleepers.

There is no mining in the province, although there have been extensive explorations for diamonds and petroleum.

The main tourist attractions in the province are water sports and fishing on the Zambezi River, the annual Kuomboka ceremony, and the annual Kazanga ceremony held in Kaoma District.

The province also has wildlife areas including national parks which are a major tourist attraction. One of them is the Liuwa Plain National Park whose history is inextricably linked with the history of the Lozi people in modern times.

The park is located west of the Barotse Floodplain of the Zambezi River near the border with Angola and was designated as a game reserve of Barotseland by the Lozi king, Lewanika, in the 1800s. It was the king's hunting area and became a national park in 1972.

Lewanika (1842–1916), also known as Lubosi Lewanika or Lewanika I, was the *Litunga* – king or paramount chief – of Barotseland from 1878 to 1916 except for a brief period in 1884-5.

He brought Barotseland – which is now the Western Province – under British control in 1890 when he agreed with Cecil Rhodes to make the region a protectorate under the British South Africa Company (BSAC).

But he later realised that he had been deceived. The terms of the agreement protected British interests to the detriment of his people. He tried to have the agreement changed but failed to do so.

Lewanika's fourth son Mbikusita reigned as *Litunga* from 1968 to 1977 as Lewanika II.

The Western Province is divided into seven districts: Kalabo, Kaoma, Lukulu, Mongu, Senanga, Secheke, and Shangombo.

The capital of Kalabo District is Kalabo. It's a small town on the plains west of the Zambezi River and the

Barotse Floodplain about 45 miles from the border with Angola.

It's located on the southeastern bank of the Luanginga River and it's the base for the Liuwa Plain National Park.

Access to Kalabo by road is difficult. The town is usually cut off during the rainy season.

The governments of Zambia and Angola also have a plan to build an inter-territorial road network which will connect the two countries by going across the floodplain. A paved highway would then be built from Kalabo northwest to the Angolan border and beyond.

Next we look at Kaoma District.

The district's capital is also known as Kaoma. It's a market town located just off the Great West Road and west of Kafue National Park.

Kaoma was previously known as Nkoya or Mankoya District before 1964.

The name Nkoya came from the first Zambian ethnic group to settle in the area. They settled there in the 700s A.D.

Besides Kaoma District, the Nkoya also live in the surrounding areas such as Mumbwa, Mulobezi, Kazungula, Mungulula (Mongu), Kalabo, and Lukulu amongst other districts.

The town of Kaoma has an 80-bed hospital serving the entire district with a population of more than 200,000.

That alone shows how bad things are, not only in Kaoma but also in other parts of Zambia in terms of development. The country has a long way to go.

Lukulu is another district in the Western Province. It's capital is also named Lukulu. It's a market town.

Lukulu District stretches across the northeastern and north-central parts of the Western Province, adjoining the North-Western Province and straddling the Zambezi River and the northern Barotse Floodplain.

The portion of the district west of the Zambezi is grassland and has no roads or towns besides dry season tracks to a few villages. But It's rich in wildlife. The Liuwa Plain National Park extends into it from the south.

Access to the town of Lukulu is limited to only a few roads which do not see much traffic.

Fish from the Zambezi form an important part of the local diet. Some of the fish are shipped to other parts of Zambia to be sold.

Lukulu is located at the northern end of the Zambezi's Barotse Floodplain. Every year between December and March, the river rises above the low banks of its main channel and spreads across the floodplain.

The town of Lukulu has a hospital, two markets and some schools.

But poor infrastructure, especially roads, impedes progress. It's very difficult to carry on trade with other parts of the country. And it's almost impossible to attract tourists to the area.

We now look at Mongu.

The capital of Mongu District is also named Mongu.

More than a quarter of the entire population of the district lives in the town of Mongu. The rest live on the floodplain or on its edge.

The population density is very low east of the Lui River because of water shortage. There is no water in that area during the dry season.

The town of Mongu was once the capital of Barotseland. And the Barotse or Lozi people were once known as the Luyi or Aluyi.

The heartland of Barotseland is the Barotse Floodplain on the upper Zambezi River, also known as Bulozi or Lyondo. But it also includes the surrounding higher ground of the plateau comprising all of what is now the Western Province.

In pre-colonial times, Barotseland included some neighbouring parts of what are now the North-Western, Central and Southern provinces as well as Caprivi in northeastern Namibia and parts of southeastern Angola beyond the Cuando River. The Cuando or Kwando River is also known as Mashi River.

Looked at another way: The influence of the Lozi nation of Barotseland spread north from what's now Botswana and Caprivi to the present-day border between Zambia and the Democratic Republic of Congo, and from southeastern Angola west to the Kafue.

The Lozi "nation" today comprises more than 25 different groups.

The traditional monarch of Barotseland – *Litunga* (king) which means "keeper or guardian of the earth" – is directly descended from the ancient Litunga Mulambwa who ruled at the turn of the 19th century. His grandson, was Lewanika I.

Historically, Barotseland's status during the advent of colonial rule differed from that of the other regions which also became part of Northern Rhodesia. It was a united independent kingdom – a well-established state – with a strong traditional ruler.

It was therefore a country by itself and would have continued to be one had it not become an integral part of the British colony of Northern Rhodesia.

Barotseland also was the first territory north of the Zambezi to sign a minerals concession and protectorate agreement with the British South Africa Company (BSAC) of Cecil Rhodes.

Although Lewanika I appealed to Queen Victoria for intervention on his behalf because the BSAC agents had misrepresented the terms of the concession, Britain proceeded to aquire the territory.

Barotseland was formally annexed as a protectorate in 1900 and became part of North-Western Rhodesia.

But it continued to lobby to be treated as a separate state and was given substantial autonomy when it became part of Northern Rhodesia and even when the country became the independent nation of Zambia.

Since its incorporation into the colony of Northern

Rhodesia, and even after the end of colonial rule, there have been strong secessionist tendencies among the Lozi, similar to what happened in Ghana where the Ashanti were strongly opposed to the unitary state instituted by President Kwame Nkrumah. It was the same situation in Uganda where the Baganda of Buganda kingdom wanted to secede when Milton Obote was Uganda's prime minister and later president.

It was in an attempt to neutralise such secessionist sentiments among the Lozi that Zambian President Kenneth Kaunda changed the name of the province from Barotseland to Western Province in 1968.

The people of Barotse claim they have been punished by the government for demanding their rights. They contend that the government has ignored Barotseland, impeding economic development in the region.

The province has only one tarred road which runs from the nation's capital Lusaka to the provincial capital Mongu. It runs in the centre of the province.

The people of the Western Province also claim that their region lacks the kind of infrastructure that's found in other provinces.

One of the biggest problems in the province is power supply. Electricity supplies are erratic, relying on an aging connection to the hydroelectric plant at Lake Kariba, the artificial lake that was created when the Kariba Dam was built in the 1950s.

All these problems have played a major role in fuelling secessionist sentiments among the Lozi even today. But although secession is a recurring theme, it's not a major problem the way it was in the sixties soon after the country won independence.

Secessionist sentiments do exist among the people of the Western Province, especially the Lozi. But such sentiments are not a pervasive phenomenon. They bubble up only from time to time.

However, they can not be ignored or be dismissed

lightly. And the provincial capital sometimes serves as a rallying point for regional heavyweights and others who articulate this position.

Located in the northern-central part of Western Province, the town of Mongu is on a promontory at higher elevation on the eastern edge of the Barotse Floodplain of the Zambezi River running north to south. During the rainy season, the river rises and sometimes floods parts of the town.

The vast majority of the people who live in Mongu are Lozi. They speak a language related to Kololo and to South African Sotho or Sesotho.

Most of the people who live in the Western Province, including non-Lozi, use Silozi as their lingua franca.

The Lozi language, or Silozi, was once known as Sikololo; a name given to the Luyi peoples by Sotho invaders known as the Makololo who crossed the Zambezi – previously known as Lyambai – in the first half of the 1800s. Their leaders were overthrown in 1864, leaving behind their language and much of their culture.

The earliest known language spoken by the Luyi people who came to the the Upper Zambezi Valley – of which Zambia's Western Province is an integral part – when they migrated from Katanga region of Congo sometime in the 1500 – 1600s – is known as Siluyana. But very few people today are able to speak or write much of the original Siluyana language.

The language was spoken by all the peoples who were absorbed into the Luyi ethno-linguistic and cultural group up to the time of the invasion of the Makololo in the late 1820s and 1830s.

The Makololo were a fairly mixed group of people by the time they moved into Barotseland but were led by a strong Sotho-speaking clan headed by their charismatic and highly respected leader, Sibituane.

By the time of the overthrow of this Sotho clan by a Luyi force led by Njekwa in 1864, the name of the Luyi had become Lozi. It was a name given to the Luyi by the Makololo. And the lingua franca of the country became Sikololo, based on Sesotho, but with considerable input from the old Siluyana language of the Luyi.

This developed over time into today's Silozi which is spoken by 700,000 people as their first language.

Most of these people live in what is now western Zambia and the Caprivi region of northeastern Namibia (the former kingdom of Barotseland).

The Lozi are also related to the Ndebele of Zimbabwe who originally came from South Africa.

The Lozi ruler, the Litunga, whohas a dry season palace about 7-and-a-half miles northwest – from Mongu – at Leauli on the floodplain, and a flood season palace on higher ground at Limulunga about 10-and-a-half miles north, is the very embodiment of the Lozi as a people and the highest expression of their collective identity. This identity is given forceful expression in the *kuomboka* ceremony every year.

The *kuomboka* ceremony which marks the court's transfer between the two locations has been described in the following terms by the Lozi themselves:

"Kuomboka is a Luyana name literally meaning 'to get out of water'. It is applied today to a traditional ceremony, which attracts more interest as a celebration of local culture each year than any other in Zambia.

It is held when the annual inundation of the Bulozi flood plain of the Upper Zambezi River reaches such a height (up to 40 feet above normal) that the Lozi Litunga or King leads his people to higher ground. This is usually at the end of March or beginning of April. The date is liable to change each year and is kept secret by the Barotse Royal establishment until close to the day.

These days, the route taken is from the village of Lealui, the capital of the Lozi Kingdom in Lewanika's time, to Limulunga, the summer or floodtime capital

151

which is where the Litunga spends most of his time today. The ceremony is preceded by heavy drumming of the royal Maoma drums, which sound of which echoes around the royal capital the day before Kuomboka, announcing the event.

In olden days the Kuomboka took place in the context of crisis as gardens and grazing were inundated and when the mounds on which so many of the inhabitants of Bulozi lived, became host to millions of rats, snakes and the fearless white ants that could consume the very buildings that people constructed to live in.

Even the snakes could not handle the ants and would hang in bushes to try to escape the attentions of the ants! The concept of Kuomboka was invented by the early Lozis as an answer to this annual problem. Not just people but cattle too had to be swum to the plain margins to graze on the harsh woodland.

During that era, people were always anxious to return to their homes on the plain but for this also, they had to wait for the Litunga who would be the one to signal the return, which is today another ceremonial occasion taking place around mid-August....The Litunga...is transported during Kuomboka...on a barge called Nalikwanda." – (Barotseland.com).

The provincial capital Mongu, which lies at the end of the 379-mile Great West Road from Lusaka, is known for basket and carpet weaving.

Mongu District also produces some of the best mangoes and fish in the country, especially the tiger fish. Mongu is also the major rice growing region of Zambia.

The town of Mongu also has a large market and an airport.

After Mongu we go to Senanga.

The headquarters of Senanga District is also called Senanga.

The town is located on the eastern bank of the

Zambezi River at the southern end of its Barotse Floodplain.

Fishng is one of the most important economic activities in Senanga.

After Senanga, we go to Sesheke which is another district in the Western Province.

The district headquarters is also called Sesheke. It's a border town and lies on the northern bank of the Zambezi River which forms the border with Namibia's Caprivi Strip at that point.

The Katima Mulilo Bridge completed in 2004 spans the river here, connecting Sesheke with the Namibian town of Katima Mulilo.

Completion of the new bridge and road was major achievement and the last missing link in the so-called "Trans-Caprivi Corridor."

The road now connects Zambia's Copperbelt with Namibia's sea port of Walvis Bay. As a result of that, the amount of road freight traffic has greatly increased. And an investment and construction boom is rapidly transforming both Sesheke and Katima Mulilo as well as surrounding areas into an economically active area critical to intet-territorial trade.

Improved road access and construction of new lodges and other tourist facilities have also increased the number of tourists passing through Sesheke on their way to Victoria Falls, Sioma Ngwezi National Park 31 miles west of the town, and to the upper Zambezi and the Barotse Floodplain.

The recent boom has also increased rural-urban migration, the growth of squatter camps near Sesheke and Katima Mulilo, and cross-border smuggling and related social problems on both sides of the Zambian-Namibian border.

Both Sesheke District and the Caprivi Region are at the bottom end of socio-economic development in their respective countries. But improvement may on the horizion if trade in the region between Zambia and Namibia continues to increase.

The last district we're going to look at in the Western Province is Shangombo. It's located in the southwestern part of the province and borders Angola.

During the Angolan civil war, the area was very dangerous because of arms smuggling. And the conflict occasionally spilled over into Zambia where villagers were killed.

A large number of Angolan refugees were placed in UN camps in the district. The largest camp was Nangweshi near the Zambezi River. It was established in 2000 for 15,000 refugees. By 2003 the district hosted about 26,000 refugees. The camps were run by the United Nations High Commission for Refugees (UNHR).

Roads in the district are often impassable during the rainy season. And vehicles can get stuck in sand during the dry season. Trucks and four-wheel-drive vehicles are the main means of transport in the area.

The area has a national park and a lot of tourist potential. Neighbouring regions in Angola and Namibia also have extensive national parks and wildlife reserves.

Wildlife in Shangombo District's own national park, Sioma Ngwezi, is still substantial in spite of poaching. And with the end of the Angolan civil war, tourism may develop in the district, facilitated by its proximity to the TransCaprivi Highway at Katima Mulilo just across the district's southern border.

The district capital, Shangombo, is just a small town. It's also one of the most remote towns in the country.

It's located on the eastern bank of the floodplain of the Cuando River. The bank forms the boundary between Zambia and Angola.

The Western Province is more than just one of the provinces of Zambia. It stands out among all the provinces as one of the most important traditional centres of power and one of the most prominent kingdoms in south-central

Africa and on the entire continent before the advent of colonial rule.

But the Lozi kingdom is an anachronistic entity in the era of modern politics which focus on integration and national unity at the expense of traditional centres of power which are more divisive than unifying in a national context because they are regionally entrenched.

Yet, in another sense, it is the pride of Zambia, and of Africa, as an example of African ingenuity which created complex institutions of authority and governance before the coming of Europeans.

The Western Province has another major asset. Because of its strategic location as a border region, it's a potential beneficiary of the inter-territorial trade which may be conducted in the future on a significant scale by the countries involved, leading to improved standards of living not only for the people of western Zambia but also for those across the borders in neighbouring countries.

After looking at all the provinces of Zambia, we're now going to look at the country's major towns and cities.

Part Four:

Major Towns and Cities

ZAMBIA'S population is one of the most urbanised in Africa. About 50 per cent of the people live in towns and cities and in other urban areas including small townships. The highest concentration is in the Lusaka area, the nation's capital.

Lusaka is not only the nation's capital; it's also the largest city in the country.

The largest urban centres in Zambia – call them towns or cities, depending on your definition – are Lusaka with a population of 3.1 million; Ndola, 748,000; Kitwe, 363,800; Kabwe, 213,800; Chingola, 150,500; Luanshya, 124,800; and Livingstone, 108,100.

These are Zambian government figures based on 2010 estimates. There are other estimates from other sources which may be different from those figures. For example, some estimates show that Mufulira has more people than Luanshya and Livingstone.

We start with the largest city, Lusaka.

Lusaka

Lusaka is the capital and largest city in Zambia. It's also the most ethnically representative part of Zambia. Every Zambian ethnic group is represented in this bustling metropolis.

Many languages are spoken in Lusaka. But the two main ones are English and Nyanja.

Bemba, the lingua franca of the Copperbelt, is also widely spoken in Lusaka.

Lusaka is located in the southern part of the central plateau of the country at an elevation of 4,196 feet. It had a population of 3,100,000 in 2007.

It's also the nation's commercial centre. And the country's four main highways – North, South, East and West – radiate from Lusaka.

As the nation's capital, Lusaka is the seat of the legislative, executive and judicial branches of government. The official residence of the president, the State House, is in Lusaka. The Parliament is in Lusaka. And the nation's highest court, the High Court, is in Lusaka.

Lusaka also is the capital of Lusaka Province, the smallest and second most populous of the country's nine provinces. Lusaka also is an administrative district run by the Lusaka City Council.

Lusaka was the site of a village named after its headman Lusaka. According to history, the village was located at Manda Hill near what's now the National Assembly – Parliament – building.

In the Nyanja language, *Manda* means "graveyard." The area was expanded by European – mostly British – settlers in 1905 when the railway was being built.

In 1935, Lusaka was chosen to replace Livingstone as the capital of the British colony of Northern Rhodesia.

The choice was determined by a number of factors: Lusaka's central location in the colony; its status as a major railway station, and for being at the crossroads of the Great North Road, the Great East Road, and the Great West Road.

After the federation of Northern Rhodesia, Southern Rhodesia and Nyasaland – known as the Federation of Rhodesia and Nyasaland or the Central African Federation – was formed in 1953, Lusaka became a hub of political activism for Africans in their quest for self-determination as a natural right.

African nationalists were opposed to the federation and demanded full independence.

When Northern Rhodesia became independent in 1964, Lusaka remained the capital. It became the capital of the new nation of Zambia.

Lusaka has also drawn many people from other parts of Zambia, including the rural areas, in search of better life. It's also a major tourist centre.

The city is also home to a large number of foreigners from many countries in and outside Africa. They include diplomats, businessmen, investors, and expatriates. Many of them also work for various organisations. Among them are religious institutions as well as non-governmental organisations commonly known as NGOs.

Lusaka also is the nation's educational centre. The highest academic institution in the country, the University of Zambia, is based in Lusaka.

The university was established in 1965. But it had its beginnings in the colleges which existed before then in Lusaka: Rhodes-Livingstone Institute, and Oppenheimer College of Social Service.

In July 1964, the former Rhodes-Livingstone Institute, a research institute with an international reputation for scholarly research and publications in the field of social anthropology dating back to 1938, came under the jurisdiction of the Provisional Council which had been formed to oversee the establishment of the University of Zambia.

In August 1965, the Oppenheimer College of Social Service was incorporated into the university.

The University of Zambia was formally established in November 1965. The first classes started in March 1966. And President Kenneth Kaunda became the university chancellor in July 1966.

The University began with three Schools: Education, Humanities and Social Sciences, and Natural Sciences. Others were added later: Law in 1967, Engineering in 1969, Medicine in 1970, Agricultural Sciences in 1971, Mines in 1973, Business and Industrial Studies at Ndola Campus in 1978, Environmental Studies also at Ndola Campus in 1981, and Veterinary Medicine at the main campus in Lusaka in 1983.

In its first academic year, the university enrolled 312 students. The numbers rose to more than 1000 in 1970. Ten years later, the university had more than 4000 students. Current enrollment stands at 11,500.

Since a very large number of students could not be accommodated at the main campus in Lusaka, it was decided in 1975 that the university should be expanded and have three campuses: one in Lusaka, another one in Ndola in the Copperbelt Province, and the third in Solwezi in the North-Western Province.

The Zambia Institute of Technology in Kitwe in the Copperbelt Province was also transformed into a full-fledged university in 1987.

Lusaka also is home to a number of other colleges and institutions of higher learning in different areas.

Lusaka also has some of the best international schools in Zambia. They include the International School of Lusaka, Rhodes Park School, Lusaka International Community School, French International School, Italian

International School, Chinese International School, Baobab College, and the American International School.

Although Rhodes Park School is not classified as an international school, it has a large number of Angolan, Nigerian, Congolese, South African, and Chinese students and others of other nationalities.

Some of the children of Zambia's elite including the children of leading politicians attend Rhodes Park School. Among them were the children of President Levy Mwanawasa and Vice President George Kunda.

The city of Lusaka has many areas of interest including national monuments and institutions.

Cairo Road is one of the main streets and points of interest in the city.

Attractions in the nation's capital include Lusaka National Museum, the Political Museum, the Zintu Community Museum, the Freedom Statue, the Zambian National Assembly, the Agricultural Society Showgrounds , the Moore Pottery Factory, the Cathedral of the Holy Cross, and the zoo and botanical gardens of the Munda Wanga Environmental Park.

Along Great East Road are the two largest shopping malls in Zambia: Arcades shopping Mall and Manda Hill shopping Mall.

Lusaka is also home to Zambia's largest airport: Lusaka International Airport. The airport is also one of Africa's largest and most important.

The airport lies on the railway line from Livingstone to Kitwe. Lusaka International Airport is used as a public and military airport.

There is also an old airport not far from the centre of the city that is no longer used by civilians but is occasionally used by the president and other high government officials.

Next we look at Ndola, the second-largest city in Zambia.

In addition to being Zambia's second-largest city,

Ndola also is the industrial, commercial, and administrative centre of the copper-mining region which is known as the Copperbelt Province.

Ndola also is the commercial capital of Zambia. And it has one of the three international airports in the country. The third one is in Livingstone in the Southern Province.

Ndola is only 6 miles from Zambia's border with the Democratic Republic of Congo. It's also the area where the airplane carrying United Nations Secretary-General Dag Hammarskjold crashed on 18 September 1961. He died in the plane crash.

The plane actually crashed near Ndola and not in Ndola itself. Dag Hammarskjold was on the way to Congo to negotiate a ceasefire between the secessionist forces of Katanga Province and UN peacekeeping troops.

There have been many reports stating that the crash was deliberate and that Hammarskjold was assassinated.

Former American President Harry Truman is reported to have said: "Dag Hammarskjöld was on the point of getting something done when they killed him. Notice that I said, 'when they killed him'."

Truman died in December 1972 more than 11 years after the crash.

A memorial was created at the crash site.

Ndola has since then gained notoriety and international attention as the place where the UN secretary-general died when he was on a peace mission to the former Belgian Congo during the turbulent sixties.

Ndola was founded in 1904 by John Edward "Chiripula" Stephenson just six months after the town of Livingstone was founded, making it the second-oldest colonial-era town in Zambia. It was started as a *boma* and as a trading post.

The Rhodesia Railways main line reached the town in 1907, carrying passengers between Ndola and other towns including Salisbury and Bulawayo in Southern Rhodesia and even Cape Town in South Africa.

The line reached the Belgian Congo, now the Democratic Republic of Congo. And from there, it was extended to the Benguela Railway which goes to the Atlantic port of Lobito Bay in Angola.

The Angolan port used to handle some of Zambia's copper exports. And it has water sufficient to allow large ships to unload close inshore.

The construction of the railway to Ndola enabled the town to develop through the years and become a major economic hub.

In fact, there was a time when Ndola was the largest industrial centre in Zambia. But the city's fortunes changed. Its economy shrunk between 1980 and 2000, reducing its economic importance.

Many factories and manufacturing firms went out of business. Ndola also had a motor vehicle assembly plant which closed down.

The city has been making slow recovery through the years but it has not regained its former glory as the nation's industrial and commercial centre even if it's still considered to be one, as it indeed is.

Ndola is the largest city on the Copperbelt. But there are no mines in Ndola itself. However, the Bwana Mkubwa open-cast mine is only 6 miles southeast of the city centre.

Although the city has no copper mines, it has played a major role in the copper industry through the years as a mineral processing centre. And it still plays an important role in the copper industry.

Copper exports provide 70 – 80 per cent of Zambia's export earnings, making the city very important to the country's economy.

Ndola also has other facilities and institutions of national importance.

The Indeni Oil Refinery in Ndola serves the whole country as a source of refined oil.

Ndola is also the headquarters of the country's leading

newspaper, the *Times of Zambia*.

One strong sign of Ndola's significance as a commercial centre of national stature is the presence of major banks in the city. Besides the capital Lusaka, Ndola is the only other city in Zambia which has the country's central bank, the Bank of Zambia. And every major bank in Zambia has at least one branch in Ndola.

Also, the largest insurance group in Zambia, ZSIC (pronounced 'zeesk'), owns many commercial and residential properties in Ndola.

Ndola also has a significant number of industries and manufacturing firms. They include beverages, brewing, distilling, manufacturing, construction and building material, ceramics, chemicals, pharmaceuticals, plastics, copper processing and refining, cobalt processing and refining, engineering, food processing, furniture manufacturing, consumer goods, glass manufacturing, metal processing and manufacturing, paint production, paper manufacturing, printing, cotton processing, textiles, and others.

Ndola also has a very large amount of limestone reserves. The limestones have their own special qualities, not found anywhere else, making them unique in the world. The limestone industry is a major source of the wealth and employment in the city.

Between 1974 and 2009, Ndola supplied more than 50 per cent of Zambia's cement. Its plant, called Chilanga Cement, was named after the location where the company was first built. It was built at Chilanga which is about 12 miles south of the nation's capital Lusaka.

Chilanga Cement has two plants in Zambia. The one at Chilanga was built in 1949; and the other one in Ndola was built in 1969.

Chilanga's largest customer is the Zambian copper industry including the large mining company ZCCM – Zambia Consolidated Copper Mines Ltd – which is the main operator of copper mines in Zambia. Chilanga

Cement also exports cement and cement clinker to neighbouring countries including Malawi, Zimbabwe and Tanzania.

A new plant was completed at Chilanga in 2008. It was expected that it would produce twice the amount of cement that was being produced at the plant in Ndola.

Limestones have proved to be a blessing for Ndola, considering the fact that the city has suffered economically through the years.

A combination of huge limestone deposits and existing transport infrastructure makes Ndola a prime destination for investment in cement and related industries.

Another important processing plant that is based on limestone in the area is Ndola Lime. It's the only producer of lime in Zambia. Lime is very important in the production of cement.

Ndola Lime also serves farmers who require agricultural lime.

Ndola also has a major airport which serves both local and international flights. It has scheduled domestic services to Lusaka and an international service to Johannesburg in South Africa and Dar es Salaam in Tanzania.

The city has several recreational parks.

One of the most memorable sites in the area is the Dag Hammarskjold Crash Site Memorial about 6 miles north of the city centre.

There was also the Dag Hammarskjold Stadium which was located on the banks of the Kafubu River south of the city. It was demolished in the 1980s in order to build a new one. But a new stadium was never rebuilt on the site. Instead, construction work began in early 2009 on a new location for the stadium

During colonial times, Ndola was a major attraction for British settlers. It had a number of good hotels such as the Savoy Hotel which was built in 1956, the Selborne Hotel and others. There was also Annesley Hotel which was later renamed Coppersmith Arms Hotel. It was located at a site that was later taken by the Royal Hotel.

Other good hotels which were highly rated in Ndola before independence included Ndola Hotel on Cecil Avenue. The street was renamed Independence Avenue after the country won independence.

In the 1950s, Rutland Hotel was rated the best hotel in Central Africa.

But Ndola has been through a lot, experiencing economic decline unprecedented in its history. Many sectors of the economy have suffered through the years. For example, when the city's industrial base suffered considerably between the 1980s and mid-2000s, the hotel and catering industry also suffered.

However, there has been a reversal in economic fortunes, with the city witnessing significant improvement in the hotel industry.

Ndola also has major historical and tourist sites. They include The Slave Tree or Mukuyu Slave Tree around which Arab slave traders carried on business transactions in the 1800s, buying and selling captured Africans.

A *mukuyu* tree is a kind of fig tree. In my native Nyakyusa language, it's called *nkuju*. There's no letter y in the Nyakyusa language just as there are no letters q, r v, x and z. In Nyakyusa, q is replaced by k, r by l, v by f, and z by s. There is no q or x in Nyakyusa or in Swahili.

Ndola also has the Copperbelt Museum with a collection of gems and minerals of the Copperbelt.

The city also has a renowned research institute, the Tropical Diseases Research Centre (TDRC) at Ndola Central Hospital. A number of research scientists conduct research in the area of tropical disease control at the institute.

Ndola also has been a symbol of decline not only in the context of Zambia but of many other parts of the African continent during the post-colonial era; a point underscored in a report by BBC appropriately entitled "The Last Shirt

Maker in Ndola":

"This year Zambia celebrates the 40th anniversary of gaining independence from Britain. It comes at a sombre time. Zambia is one of the large group of African countries which has become poorer in recent years.

'Get ready for a bumpy ride,' said Sury Patel, as he hunched over the wheel of his 18-year-old Nissan, turning into Independence Way, the main street of Ndola.

You would not have known that we were in a city of half a million people, in the industrial heartland of Zambia. Forty years after independence, Independence Way looks the worse for wear.

It was a narrow road, pitted with holes in the tarmac and with no streetlights to help Mr Patel as he jolted along, peering through the cracked windscreen of his car.

We were heading for a drink at the cricket club where Mr Patel was secretary, as he was of the city's masonic lodge, its main school board, a hospital and several other causes as well.

'There is not an institution in Ndola which I have not been secretary of,' he said, in imitation of the Mikado's Pooh-Ba, as he ordered Rhino beers and settled into a bar stool.

Collapsing industries

The Ndola cricket club was a single-storey, white painted building with a corrugated iron roof and a polished screed floor. It was built some 60 years ago or so and had a comforting architectural familiarity to anyone who has travelled in former British colonies in Africa.

But, like so much else in Zambia, cricket is dying. In Ndola, it is dead already.

'There is no cricket played here any more,' Mr Patel complained, as he remembered the days when his slow bowling had been a feature of the team.

167

The main copper mine nearby has gone, taking the town's copper refinery with it, and the textile industry has collapsed too. Mr Patel's shirt factory is one of the few still open and he employs only 20 people where he used to employ 200. The closures were inevitable once other industries declined.

It does not take an economic genius to work out that, if most of the purchasers of your shirts lose their jobs, then they can no longer afford to buy them.

But another plague hit the textile factories too. Just as they were losing their domestic market, Zambia was forced to open its borders to imports.

Painful prescription

The order came from the International Monetary Fund, as part of the so-called structural adjustment which these gatekeepers of globalisation demand as the entrance price to the world economy.

The IMF's textbook prescribes short-term pain to make long-term gain. Countries have to open their borders to the chill winds of competition, while removing subsidies from their own industries.

The textbook says that foreign investment will then flood in, opening new competitive industries to replace those that have collapsed. It has not worked in Zambia, at least not yet.

During the period of the most intense IMF-led reforms, it has tumbled more than 30 places down the UN's index of poverty. It is now one of the 12 poorest countries in the world.

Mr Patel simply cannot compete with the cheap second-hand clothing which now fills the markets of Ndola.

The IMF's programme has had another effect too. Foreign companies taking over Zambian factories were given lucrative tax breaks.

There was nothing to stop them taking their tax breaks, stripping out the factories and closing them down, in order to sell goods into Zambia from their plants in neighbouring countries. Not that many Zambians have much money to buy anything any more.

There are signs of decay everywhere across the country. In Livingstone, next to the Victoria Falls, around 20,000 people have lost their jobs in the last ten years.

'Mad waste'

There is huge potential for tourism here, which they have hardly begun to exploit. And amid the industrial wasteland of closed factories, there is now a grain storehouse.

It is a mad waste of resources in a town which should be able to feed itself on the proceeds of tourism. The Victoria Falls are a World Heritage Site, but they should not need the World Food Programme to stay alive.

Back in the cricket club in Ndola, the other men at the bar - all Zambian businessmen of Asian extraction - had a number of different answers to the country's problems.

The socialism of the country's first 25 years was blamed, as well as corruption. But they all conceded that socialism had protected their ability to make money in the early years, and corruption in Zambia is much less damaging than in many African countries.

The country has amazing tourist potential. It has a benevolent climate and has never had a war. Perhaps the IMF's textbook ideas did not work after all.

Mr Patel is not waiting to find out. His three children are now in the United States. His eldest son, who is a trained accountant, wanted to come back to Zambia.

He was prepared to take a pay cut, but not down to the one-tenth of his US earnings which was all he would have made here.

As soon as he can get the right visa, Mr Patel - the last

shirt maker in Ndola - is going to join his family in America and Zambia will be the poorer for him going." – (David Loyn, in his report from Ndola, Zambia, "The Last Shirt Maker in Ndola," BBC News, Saturday, 22 May 2004).

But there are better days ahead, not only for Ndola and for Zambia as a country but for Africa as a whole.

After Ndola, we look at Kitwe.

Kitwe is the third-largest city in Zambia. It's also one of the most developed commercial and industrial areas in the nation, alongside Ndola and Lusaka, with a complex of mines on its northwestern and western edges.

Kitwe is located close to the border with the Democratic Republic of Congo. It has a number of townships and suburbs including Nkana East, Nkana West, Mindolo and Garneton. The city is sometimes referred to as Kitwe-Nkana.

Kitwe also has one of the largest mines in Africa: Nkana Mine. It's a copper mine located a little more than half a mile southwest of Kitwe. It's an underground mine and an open pit which has been in operation since 1932. It has produced 6 million tonnes of copper so far.

Kitwe was founded in 1936 in north-central Northern Rhodesia as the railway was being built by Cecil Rhodes' British South Africa Company (BSAC). It was first established as part of a copper-mining centre at Nkana.

The expanding copper mines at Nkana made it the dominant centre in the region and Kitwe started growing in size and significance over the years, finally surpassing Nkana as the main centre.

Kitwe has three institutions of higher learning: Copperbelt University (CBU), a public university that was once part of the University of Zambia (UNZA) but became a separate institution in 1987. It's one of the biggest universities in the country.

Then there is Copperstone University, and the Zambia

Institute of Business Studies and Industrial Practice.

The city also has a number of manufacturing plants including beverages, ceramics, chemicals, engineering, plastics, food processing, textiles and others.

The vast majority of the people in Kitwe are Christian as is the case with most in Zambian towns and cities as well as in other parts of the country. But there are smaller groups of other believers as well, including Hindus, Muslims, Sikhs, Buddhists, Jews and others.

Kitwe also has one of the largest numbers of Europeans and people of European descent in Zambia.

Among Zambians, the Bemba are the dominant group in Kitwe. Other groups include the Chewa, Lozi, Tonga, Mambwe, Lunda, Kaonde, and immigrants such as the Nyakyusa from neighbouring Tanzania, a group to which I belong.

Next we go to Kabwe.

Kabwe is the fourth-largest city in Zambia. Located in the Central Province, it has literally played a central role in the evolution and life of Zambia from a colony to an independent nation.

Formerly known as Broken Hill, it was founded when the Broken Hill lead and zinc deposits were discovered in 1902.

Kabwe also has a claim to being the birthplace of Zambian politics.

The name Kabwe or Kabwe-Ka Mukuba means "ore" or "smelting." But instead of using an African name, European and Australian mineral hunters named it after a similar mine in Broken Hill in New South Wales, Australia.

The mine became the largest in Northern Rhodesia until it was overtaken in the early 1930s by larger copper mining complexes on the Copperbelt.

Apart from lead and zinc, the mine in Broken Hill also produced silver, manganese, and heavy metals such as cadmium, vanadium and titanium in smaller quantities.

In 1921. a human fossil – a skull – which was later named Broken Hill Man or Rhodesian Man, was found in the mine; other sources say in a cave.

The remains of an extinct hominid which is also referred to as Kabwe Cranium were found by a miner.

Until that time, it was the oldest hominid fossil ever found. Also known as the Kabwe Skull or Broken Hill Skull, the cranium was found by Tom Zwiglaar, a Swiss miner, in a lead and zinc mine.

The mine, which occupies a one-and-a-half square-mile area just a little more than half a mile southwest of the town centre, is now closed. But metals are still extracted from old tailings.

Kabwe is also one of the most polluted places in Zambia because discharges from the mine end up polluting the water in the city.

The first railway in the country operated by Rhodesian Railways – when the territory was administered as North-Western Rhodesia and North-Eastern Rhodesia – reached the Broken Hill mine in 1906. And the town became the northern operational base for the railway. After the mining industry, the railway became the second-biggest employer in the whole country.

A locomotive maintenance facility was built in Broken Hill and, in 1909, the railway reached Ndola in a region that came to be known as the Copperbelt in the late 1920s after the discovery of very large quantities of copper.

The railway workers' unions played a large role in politics in Northern Rhodesia. The country was a British colony in which Africans did not have equal rights. And white workers wanted to protect their privileged status they enjoyed at the expense of blacks.

In racially-segregated colonial times before Africans had the right to vote, the town of Broken Hill was the seat of Roy Welensky, the leader of the powerful Rhodesia Railway Workers Union (RRWU). He later became prime minister of the Federation of Rhodesia and Nyasaland.

The federation was opposed by the Northern Rhodesia Railway Trade Union which was the labour union of black railway workers. The union was led by Dixon Konkola. Like the railway union for white workers led by Welensky, the black union was also based in Broken Hill.

Its leader, Dixon Konkola, was one of the leading nationalists in the struggle for independence. But he also came to be one of the most forgotten. Yet his place is in Zambian history is guaranteed.

When one of the leading African nationalist parties, the Zambian African National Congress (ZANC), was proscribed in 1959, Konkola was one of the leaders who formed other political parties to carry on the struggle.

The ZANC was a breakaway from the African National Congress (ANC) led by Harry Nkumbula. ZANC leaders felt that the ANC was not radical enough to lead the struggle for independence. After the ZANC was banned, Dixon Konkola formed the African National Freedom Movement. As Assa Okoth states in his book, *A History of Africa: African Nationalism and The De-colonisation Process*:

"Simon Kapwewe, a friend of Kaunda's from Lubwa, Munukayumbwa Sipalo and Sikota Wina – young men who had emerged from secondary schools and obtained further education from overseas – now found Nkumbula's leadership too moderate, and were committed to the idea of creating an independent African state.

This aim, they believed, could only be achieved by refusing to compromise in any way with the federal political system.

Kenneth Kaunda, who had been Secretary-General of the Congress since 1953, very neatly expressed this ideal. Nkumbula, the president of the ANC, was clearly less committed to their radical approach. As a matter of fact, he was known to be associating with whites; it was Harry Franklin, a white member of the Executive Council, who had persuaded Nkumbula to call off the boycott of the white trading areas to give the Race Relations Board 'a chance.'

'We will do our best to work for the development of Northern Rhodesia and all its people,' he said, 'but for this we need the help and sympathy of all the liberal-minded Europeans.'

Nkumbula's attitude was underlined when he accepted the constitution of September 1958. While the radical leaders were against this constitution, Nkumbula not only accepted it, but also said that he would stand in the forthcoming elections as an ANC candidate.

As well as fraternising with the whites, Nkumbula was also spending a lot of the party's money and refusing to let Kapwepwe, the Treasurer, keep proper accounts. Furthermore, Nkumbula went to London but failed, for dubious reasons, to keep an appointment with the Colonial Secretary; it was felt he was going to give the Nationalist Movement a bad name.

He also demanded dictatorial powers within the ANC and dismissed branch officials who were not loyal. The younger men felt, therefore that they had no alternative but to break away and form a party of their own.

On October 26, 1958, the Zambian African National Congress (ZANC) was formed. Kaunda was president, Kapwewe Treasurer-General, and Sipalo Seceretary-General.

Other members were the Lozi journalist Sikota Wina, and Bemba businessmen Grey Zulu and Lewis Changufu.

ZANC had support in the Northern Province, the Copperbelt and Eastern Province. Outside Zambia it quickly gained support from world leaders such as Nkrumah and Nasser. Nkumbula's support was now restricted mainly to Zambia's Southern Province (Nkumbula's home region dominated by his people the Tonga and the Ila).

The radical leaders, led by Kenneth Kaunda, had

vowed they would have nothing to do with the elections held to be held in April 1959.

In February and March of that year there were disturbances in Malawi (Nyasaland) and, fearing that the trouble might spread to Zambia (Northern Rhodesia), Governor Benson decided to act quickly.

Before dawn on March 12, 1959, ZANC officials and 45 of their supporters were taken into custody. Kaunda was first sent to Kabompo, then to prisons in Salisbury and Lusaka. Kapwepwe was sent to Morigu, Wina's home district, and Wina was sent to Luwingu, Kapwepwe's home district; this was to separate the leaders from their supporters.

There was violence at Chilubi Island in Lake Bangweulu and in other parts of the Northern and Luapula Provinces. More than 100 Africans were arrested. The election itself passed off peacefully, Nkumbula winning his seat for ANC in company with 13 members of the United Federal Party and four of the Central Africa Party.

ZANC was proscribed, but other parties immediately emerged. In May 1959, Barry Banda, Dauti Yamba and Paskale Sokota founded the African National Freedom Movement. Dixon Konkola, president of the Railway Workers Union, founded the United African Congress. In June 1959, these two parties combined to form the United National Freedom Party.

A third party, the African National Independence Party was formed by Paul Kalichini. In September 1959, this joined with the United National Freedom Party to form the United National Independence Party (UNIP).

The ANC was meanwhile doing badly. Between June and September 1959, a split had developed between Nkumbula and Titus Mukupo. Fines Bulawayo and a British-trained barrister, Mainza Chona, supported Mukupo. In October 1959, Chona, Bulawayo and Mukupo left the ANC and joined UNIP.

In January 1960 Kaunda was released from o prison;

he took over the leadership of UNIP as its president, with Kapwewe as vice-president. Together, Kaunda and Kapwepwe now turned their attention to the organisation of the party.

Kaunda was in a very good position to play an effective role in this. In 1957, he had spent six months in Britain studying the organisation of the British Labour Party. He had also studied the CPP (Convention People's Party) in Ghana. The organisation of UNIP was a combination of these two.

By 1962, UNIP had 23 regional organisations, 67 constituencies, 986 branches and over 6,500 workers.

The party's aim was majority rule and self-government through 'non-violent means plus positive action.' This again shows the influence of Nkrumah, together with that of Mahatma Gandhi. Kaunda following closely the example of Gandhi emphasised that the struggle was against imperialism and colonialism, not against their agents. Despite this non-violence stance, however, there was a certain amount of violence in 1960.

UNIP was a mass party and adopted slogans such as 'one m,an one vote' that would appeal to the masses. The strategy was to work for constitutional changes that would bring about African majority rule in Zambia, enabling Zambia to leave the federation and finally achieve the ultimate goal of independence. Kaunda made proposals along these lines in 1959 and again in March 1960. He also visited London. Accra and Dar es Salaam to gain support."– (Assa Okoth, *A History of Africa: African Nationalism and The De-colonisation Process*, Nairobi, Kenya: East African Publishers, 2006, pp. 108 – 110).

The town of Kabwe played a major in the evolution of these events in the struggle for independence.

Although many leaders in the independence movement came from many other parts of Northern Rhodesia, there is no question that Kabwe – former Broken Hill – stands out among all the places which produced nationalist leaders and fuelled the nationalist struggle for independence as the birth place of Zambian nationalism.

Today the town is the headquarters of Zambia Railways. But employment levels on the railway have been heavily cut back.

Reflecting its central location and railway union base, Kabwe emerged as the choice by African nationalist leaders for a rally which was held on 26 October 1958 at Mulungushi Rock north of the city. Kabwe was then just a town and still known as Broken Hill.

The rally was held by the Zambian African National Congress led by Kenneth Kaunda. After Kaunda and his colleagues including Simon Kapwepwe later founded the United National Independence Party (UNIP), they continued to hold conferences at Mulungushi Rock. Mulungushi Rock later came to be known as the "birthplace of independence"'in Zambia.

The name of the town was changed from Broken Hill to Kabwe in 1966 shortly after independence.

The city has seen good and bad times. For example, when the mine was closed, the city witnessed economic decline as it did when many railway workers also lost their jobs.

Kabwe has a number of manufacturing industries including the Zambia-China Mulungushi Textiles plant built with the help of the Chinese in the 1980s. Other industries include pharmaceuticals, milling and cotton ginning, and leather tanning.

Commercial farming areas surround Kabwe about 6 miles from the city centre. And road and rail links provide access to markets of the Copperbelt and the nation's capital Lusaka.

To the east and west of Kabwe are areas with good tourist potential, together with the advantages of Kabwe's central location – virtually as the geographical centre of the country – and its proximity to Lusaka. Kabwe also has an international airport, a major asset for tourism.

Notable places and attractions in Kabwe include the Mulungushi Rock Authority which is located north of the city; Bwacha House National Monument where Kenneth Kaunda was elected president of the Zambian African National Congress (ZANC) on 8 March 1958; Big Tree National Monument which is a fig tree with a 165-foot wide canopy which served as a meeting place on many occasions during the early years of the town's history; and Kwame Nkrumah Teachers Training College, among others.

Kabwe is also the birth place of best-selling novelist Wilbur Smith. He was born in the town of Broken Hill on 9 January 1933 in what was then the British colony of Northern Rhodesia.

He's one of Zambia's most well-known authors and probably its most acclaimed novelist. He's also the pride of Kabwe as its native son.

Like other parts of Zambia, Kabwe has had its ups and downs. But whatever the town has gone through, it has never lost its status as the birthplace of the independence movement.

Its name is a symbol of national pride, indelibly etched in the nation's memory to be cherished for generations to come. As one Zambian journalist, Kelvin Kachingwe, stated in his article, "Kabwe: The Nucleus Of National Politics," published in the *Times of Zambia*:

"Other than the town being centrally located, Kabwe has often hosted meetings whose outcome or resolutions have gone on to influence the political landscape of the country.

Simply put, Kabwe has a special place in the history of this country. You can call the former mining town a nucleus of national politics, if you like.

And it all started when first republican president Dr Kenneth Kaunda and his childhood friend and former vice-president Simon Mwansa Kapwepwe and their group resigned from the Harry Mwaanga Nkumbula-led African National Congress (ANC) to form the short-lived Zambia African National Congress (ZANC).

It was in fact, on October 26, 1958, that the breakaway Kaunda-Kapwepwe group, travelled to Kabwe to address the first rally which is said to have been a success in that it sent shock waves to the colonial administration.

At that time, Kabwe was considered to be the nucleus of national politics because it was Roy Welensky's United Federal Party (UFP) seat.

Welensky, the former prime minister of the Federation of Rhodesia and Nyasaland who was nicknamed Mazambani, lived there and led a powerful European Railway Workers Union (ERWU).

The ERWU for white employees of Rhodesia Railways was very strong in Southern Rhodesia (Zimbabwe) and this made Roy Welensky a force to reckon with. Little wonder when it came to find a person for the position of Prime Minister for the Federation of Rhodesia and Nyasaland, Welensky was the automatic choice.

Welensky, who later resigned from Rhodesia Railways, formed the United Federal Party and won the support of the powerful European Mineworkers Union (EMU).

Ironically, Kabwe was also the seat for one of the biggest trade unions in the land - the Northern Rhodesia Railway Trade Union under the strong leadership of Dixon Konkola.

Some leaders of the ANC like Grey Zulu, who later became UNIP's longest serving secretary-general, Paul Kalichini, who had now moved to Kabwe, and Raphael Kombe, were at the helm of the party in the centrally located mining town.

Having addressed a public meeting on October 26, the ANC-breakaway faction officially launched ZANC from Kabwe, which was also known as Bethlehem, after the birthplace of the Lord Jesus Christ.

179

Unlike the ANC, the newly formed ZANC posed a very serious threat to the colonial administration forcing them to ban the party a few months after its formation. Its leaders were also arrested or restricted in areas far away from their homes.

But far from quitting, the ZANC leaders went on to form the United National Independence Party (UNIP), which together with the ANC went on to win the political independence for the country. UNIP, whose birthplace was Kabwe also went on to rule the country for 27 years, and was only dislodged by the ruling Movement for Multi-Party Democracy (MMD).

And as if by providence, the ruling MMD, whose initial formation, stemmed from a meeting at Garden House motel, was to be officially launched in Kabwe at Kasandamalonde.

The formation and launch of MMD turned out to be the first serious challenge to UNIP's hold on power in close to three decades. Shortly after its formation, the MMD went on to claim a memorable victory against the UNIP government in the presidential and parliamentary elections of 1991.

The MMD has gone on to rule the country to date suffering what sometimes appeared like irreparable damage in the process. These include the initial resignation of some founding members like Arthur Wina, Emmanuel Kasonde, Humphrey Mulemba, Baldwin Nkumbula, Akashambatwa Mbikusita-Lewanika to form the National Party (NP) and the late Dean Namulya Mung'omba and Mbita Chitala, who formed the Zambia Democratic Congress (ZDC). These incidents happened in the first term of the MMD's rule while in the second and final term of Dr Frederick Chiluba as party president, it again suffered some damage especially when the third term debate emerged.

The debate resulted in the split with a good number of their members of Parliament being expelled. In fact, three major political parties emerged out of the ashes of the third term debate, namely the Republican Party led by Ben Mwila, the Forum for Democracy and Development (FDD) and the Heritage Party (HP).

The FDD was to five years later to go back to Kabwe for its mid-term convention. And like most political meetings held in Kabwe, the FDD affair proved somewhat controversial if not decisive with the election of Munali MP and former Finance Minister, Edith Nawakwi as president, replacing Lieutenant General Christon Tembo who retired from active politics.

Nawakwi became the first woman to be popularly elected president of a political party in the country.

And as if to follow tradition, Dr Nevers Mumba in forming his National Citizens Coalition (NCC) in 1997, chose Kasanda grounds in Kabwe as the venue for the official launch of the party whose membership was primarily drawn from the Christian community.

But although it is the main town of Kabwe that has sometimes gained recognition for hosting these important functions, the Mulungushi Rock of Authority, an obscure location comprising a cluster of rocks near the banks of Mulungushi river 10 kilometres from Kabwe, should in fact take a lot of credit. In fact, the Mulungushi Rock of Authority deserves to be called the living memory of Zambia's nationalism since it was the exact birthplace of ZANC.

Other than that, it has hosted some of the most controversial meetings in living memory of Zambia with one of the most indelible ones being the 1967 UNIP council meeting at which Simon Mwansa Kapwepwe announced his candidature for the position of vice-president of the party.

The announcement of his candidature pitted him against Reuben Kamanga, and to some (in fact large) extent also caught Dr Kaunda by surprise. Other than that, it also brought out in the open the tribal divisions that existed in UNIP with two factions emerging to support Kapwepwe on one hand and Kamanga on the other.

This is the same meeting that led to the resignation of Dr Kaunda as president for a few hours. Veteran politician and journalist Sikota Wina refers to this time as 'the night without a president' in his book.

However, despite Kapwepwe winning the vice-presidency, UNIP was never the same again. In fact, barely two years after his victory, Kapwepwe resigned as vice-president of both the party and the republic saying his tribesmen were being victimised. He later formed the short-lived United Progressive Party (UPP).

Two decades or so later, UNIP went back to the Rock of Authority for another council meeting at which former republican vice president Enock Kavindele announced that he would be challenging Dr Kaunda for the presidency of the party.

That announcement was not welcomed by many UNIP members especially the women who thought Kavindele was insulting Dr Kaunda by challenging him. And because of the pressure, Kavindele pulled out of the race after which he formed his own party before joining the MMD.

Kavindele has himself confessed that the atmosphere at the Rock of Authority was intense such that he had to wear a bulletproof for fear of being shot.

Kavindele returned to the Rock of Authority a decade later to contest the MMD Vice Presidency pitting him against the late Paul Tembo.

The convention as a whole, and the elections for the position of Vice-President in particular, proved controversial. It is also at this same convention that the likes of Brigadier-General Godfrey Miyanda and Lieutenant-General Christon Tembo were refused entry.

In the end, the convention managed to amend the party constitution to allow Frederick Chiluba a third term.

In the next few weeks, the MMD will be returning to the Rock of Authority for its convention at which new party leaders are expected to be ushered in. Already, one Dr Nevers Mumba, a presidential aspirant, is a casualty having been expelled from the ruling party even before he could file-in his nomination papers. Such is the character of the Rock of Authority. But as to whether the MMD will live-up to the historical character of the Rock, it is a wait-and-see situation.

But even if it does not, Kabwe and indeed, the Mulungushi Rock of Authority is a bedrock of Zambian politics." – (Kelvin Kachingwe, "Kabwe: The Nucleus of National Politics," in *Times of Zambia*, Ndola, Zambia, March 2007).

From Kabwe, we go to Chingola, the fifth-largest city in Zambia.

Located on the Copperbelt, or in the Copperbelt Province, Chingola has the distinction of being home to the second-largest open-cast mine in the world: Nchanga Open Pit Mine.

Chingola was founded somewhat later than the cities in the southeastern half of the Copperbelt, in 1943, when the Nchanga Open Pit was started. It was once known to be the cleanest town in Zambia.

Chingola also has an underground mine.

A freight-only branch of Zambia Railways serves the town from Kitwe.

From Chingola we go to Mufulira.

Mufulira grew up in the 1930s around the site of the Mufulira copper mine on its northwestern edge.

The city is located about 10 miles from Zambia's border with the Democratic Republic of Congo (DRC). It's also the starting point of the Congo Pedicle road which connects the Copperbelt to the Luapula Province, making that province Mufulira's commercial hinterland.

A tarred highway to the southwest connects Mufulira to Kitwe which is about 25 miles away, and Chingola, 34 miles away. Another road to the southeast goes to Ndola, the commercial and transport hub of the Copperbelt, about 62 miles away. A branch of Zambia Railways, carrying freight only, serves the mine in Mufulira.

Production at the Mufulira Mine is down from the 1969 peak when the Copperbelt made Zambia the world's fourth-largest producer of copper.

Mufulira is also known as the birthplace of Zambia's President Levy Mwanawasa. He served as president from 2002 until his death in 2008 at the age of 59.

Another major urban centre on the Copperbelt and in the country as a whole is Luanshya.

Luanshya was founded in the early part of the 20th century after a prospector/explorer, William Collier, shot and killed a Roan Antelope on the banks of the Luanshya River, discovering a copper deposit in the process.

It's said that when the antelope fell to the ground, its head ended up resting on a rock where an exposed seam of copper ore could be clearly seen. The mining company that was later formed to dig up the copper in the area was named "Roan Antelope Copper Mines Ltd."

For most of the 20th century, copper was mined in great quantities at Luanshya. But towards the end of the century, mining became expensive, without enough returns to justify the investment in the venture. The result was severe economic problems for Luanshya, a town that was founded, survived, and thrived on copper mining.

But there are still significant quantities of copper underground in Luanshya.

Whether or not the town sees a revival in its fortunes and regains its former glory as one of the main mining centres on the Copperbelt will depend on how efficiently this mineral is extracted and sold.

Farther away from the Coperbelt is Livingstone in the southern part of the country.

Livingstone is a historic colonial city and capital of the Southern Province. It's also a tourism centre and the main gateway to Victoria Falls. It's a border town located about 6 miles north of the Zambezi River and has road and rail connections to Zimbabwe on the other side of the Falls.

There is also a historic place called Mukuni located about 6 miles to the southeast of Livingstone. It was the largest village in the area before the town of Livingstone was founded.

In 1855, Dr. David Livingstone became the first European to explore the Zambezi River in what is now the Livingstone area.

In the 1890s, Cecil Rhodes and his British South Africa Company (BSAC) established imperial rule north of the Zambezi River. He started looking for minerals and was involved in other commercial activities in what came to be known as North-Western Rhodesia.

The main crossing point on the Zambezi River was above the falls at a place called the Old Drift.

As the Old Drift crossing became more used, a settlement was established there. Around 1897, the settlement became the first municipality in the country. It's sometimes referred to as "Old Livingstone."

But the European settlers were forced to abandon the settlement because it was close to mosquito breding areas. Many people died from malaria.

After 1900, the settlers moved to higher ground and established a settlement. As the settlement grew, it became a town. The town was named Livingstone in honour of the missionary-explorer Dr. David Livingstone.

The town of Livingstone grew fast. It also enjoyed economic prosperity, prompting the British South Africa Company to move the capital there in 1907.

In 1911, the British South Africa Company merged the territory of North-Western Rhodesia with North-Eastern Rhodesia to form Northern Rhodesia.

Livingstone prospered from its position as a gateway to trade between the northern and southern sides of the Zambezi. It also prospered from farming in the Southern

Province – where it's located – and from commercial timber production in forests to the northwestern part of the town.

It was an era of prosperity and a number of colonial buildings were erected during that period. And they still stand today.

The capital of Northern Rhodesia was moved from Livingstone to Lusaka in 1935 to be closer to the economic heartland of the Copperbelt industries based on copper, timber, hides, tobacco, cotton and other agricultural products.

But Livingstone remained a prosperous town. The town of Victoria Falls in Southern Rhodesia had the tourist trade, but many supplies were bought from Livingstone.

Of all the towns in Northern Rhodesia, colonial Livingstone took on the character of Southern Rhodesia or South Africa at that time. It was heavily segregated, although colour bar – racial discrimination – was not sanctioned as official policy as was the case in apartheid South Africa. Still, the result was the same.

The northern and western halves of Livingstone and the town centre were reserved for the colonial government and white-owned businesses and residential areas for whites. And the eastern and southern parts were for blacks. A black township even grew in the area. It was named Maramba after the small Maramba River which flows near the place.

Asians and people of mixed race owned businesses and lived in the middle on the eastern side of the town's centre. And they were treated better than blacks.

As independence approached and for a few years after the end of colonial rule, many whites in Livingstone left and moved to Rhodesia or South Africa, refusing to mix and live with blacks and under black majority rule.

After independence, Livingstone benefited from the financial resources of the new government of Zambia which were spent on a number of development projects in town. Livingstone also benefited from tourism and from the money spent by the large number of expatriates who had been employed to assist in those projects.

Livingstone even benefited from spending by black Africans who were now experiencing for the first time the freedom they never enjoyed during colonial rule when they were treated as second-class citizens or not as citizens at all in their native land.

But things changed in the late sixties. After the white minority settlers in Rhodesia unilaterally declared independence, what came to be known as the Unilateral Declaration of Independence (UDI) in November 1965, Zambia closed the border. And the town of Livingstone suffered a lot.

The town suffered economically due to a decline in tourism and loss of trade after the Zambian-Rhodesian border was closed. Also, the timber industry ended as the forests around Mulobezi were used up. Manufacturing firms also suffered because of poor management.

All this was exacerbated – in the '70s ans '80s – by the nation's economic problems which were partly caused by low copper prices, poor economic management, and wrong economic policies.

Things had gone so bad that even when trade to the south was re-started following Zimbabwe's independence in 1980, Livingstone still could not take full advantage of the new economic opportunities which had now become available in the newly independent Zimbabwe.

But since the end of the 1990s, Livingstone has experienced a resurgence in tourism at Zimbabwe's expense because of the turmoil in that country.

However the town has also come under considerable pressure following the decline in the nation's copper industry and in some agricultural sectors. Many people have moved into town, far more than the town can accommodate in terms of employment and even housing. This has caused a lot of problems for Livingstone.

Crime has gone up. The environment has suffered because of waste problems. And competition for scarce jobs has reached unprecedented levels, fuelling clashes and even leading to family disintegration.

Apart from tourism, the other hope for Livingstone is development stimulated by the Walvis Bay Corridor with the opening of the Katima Mulilo Bridge and completion of the Trans-Caprivi Highway 120 miles east which funnels more trade through the town.

The Walvis Bay Corridor will bring together different transport systems and other infrastructural facilities in the countries in the region to coordinate and facilitate trade for their collective wellbeing, with Walvis Bay in Namibia serving as a major outlet to the sea.

All these links will converge on Walvis Bay. Zambia as a country, and Livingstone in particular, will greatly benefit from all this because of its strategic location.

And if there is to be a local name for the town of Livingstone, it's "Maramba."

The name predates Livingstone. It's the name of the river flowing on the eastern outskirts of Livingstone and the large township next to it.

The name is used for a number of places and features in Livingstone and has been proposed as the new or as an alternative name for the city as a whole.

In fact, "Livingstone" is the only non-African name for a town or city in Zambia that has not been changed since independence.

One of the reasons given for the preservation of this colonial legacy is reportedly Kenneth Kaunda's fondness for the name. Whether this is true or not, we'll never know. But it's attributed to him.

It's said that President Kaunda did not want the name changed because his father – who came from Nyasaland as did Kenneth Kaunda's mother – was educated by Scottish missionaries who followed in Dr. Livingstone's footsteps. And he wanted the name kept in memory of his father and in honour of those missionaries and Dr. Livingstone himself.

Some people already call Livingstone – "Maramba." But they have a lot of work to do to convince the authorities to change the name officially.

Livingstone is heavily dependent on tourism. And its name has international recognition as a major tourist destination. Any change of name will adversely affect tourism since many people who want to visit Livingstone, and Victoria Falls, don't know any other name for the town besides "Livingstone."

The town has also enjoyed success in tourism in recent years. Therefore it's obvious that any suggestion to change the name of the town will be strongly resisted by business owners and employees who benefit from tourism. There's no question that the change would affect recognition of the town as an international tourist destination.

If the name is changed to Maramba, people will be asking - "Where is Maramba?" But if you ask them, "Where is Livingstone?" They will tell you, "Zambia," or "Victoria Falls."

And it's very much possible, may be even highly probable, that tourism may grow exponentially in Livingstone in the coming years.

There are many important sites and activities in and around Livingstone for tourists and other people. They include Victoria Falls which is protected and served by the Mosi-oa-Tunya National Park on the city's southwestern edge; wildlife safaris – game drives – in the wildlife section of the Mosi-oa-Tunya National Park; and birdwatching in the Mosi-oa-Tunya National Park.

Other attractions are Batoka Gorges below Victoria Falls in the Mosi-oa-Tunya National Park; Zambezi River above the Falls including river cruises, sports fishing, kayaking; Victoria Falls Field Museum featuring geology and archaeology around the Falls; and flights over the Falls.

There is also the Livingstone Museum which is devoted to archaeology, ethnography and history and contains a magnificent collection of memorabilia relating to David Livingstone.

In front of the museum there is a statue in memory of Dr. David Livingstone erected in 2005. There is another statue, also erected in 2005, in honour of Czech explorer and ethnographer, Emil Holub, who made the first detailed map of the region surrounding Victoria Falls in 1875. Holub also wrote and published the first book account of the Victoria Falls published in English in Grahamstown, South Africa, in 1879.

Other places of interest in Livingstone include the Maramba Cultural Centre featuring traditional dancing, singing, costumes; Mukuni Village with its annual Lwiindi Ceremony held in July; Victoria Falls Bridge; and the Railway Museum of the Mulobezi Railway.

The city of Livingstone also has Saint Andrews Church built in1910-11 in memory of Dr. David Livingstone and still in use; Old Government House which was the main government office and governor's residence (1907-1935) when Livingstone was the capital of North-Western Rhodesia and North-Eastern Rhodesia; and craft markets such as Mukuni Victoria Falls Craft Village.

Livingstone is indeed a historic city. And it's a powerful reminder of a bygone era.

It's the eighth-largest city in Zambia but, in terms of history, it's the most prominent as the embodiment of the era of British imperial glory in Northern Rhodesia.

The ninth-largest urban centre in Zambia is Kasama which we have already looked at when we learned about the Northern Province.

It's classified as a city. But it can also be called a town, not a city, depending on one's definition of "city" and "town." It's really not large enough to be a city. But it's well-known in Zambia because it's the capital of the Northern Province.

The tenth-largest urban centre in Zambia is Chipata. It's also no more than a town and is the capital of the Eastern Province as we learned earlier.

There are many other towns in Zambia. But the ones we have just looked at are the largest urban centres in one of the most urbanised countries on the African continent.

Even when Northern Rhodesia won independence as Zambia in October 1964, it was already one of the most urbanised colonial territories in Africa mainly because of the industrialisation of the Copperbelt which led to the growth and development of large urban centres in that region.

It became the most industrialised area in the country. And it still is one today. It's the pulse of the nation in a country full of life.

CPSIA information can be obtained at www.ICGtesting.com
Printed in the USA
BVOW031035291012

304195BV00001B/31/P